G000123000

RAY CHARLES

Ray Charles's command of the blues has made him one of the most popular performers of our time.

DR. JOHN

Dr. John is well-known for including great blues piano into his unique New Orleans-style music.

Introduction to the Blues

Four Easy Steps to Teach Yourself to Play the Blues

- **STEP 1:**

  THE THREE BASIC CHORDS USED TO PLAY THE C BLUES

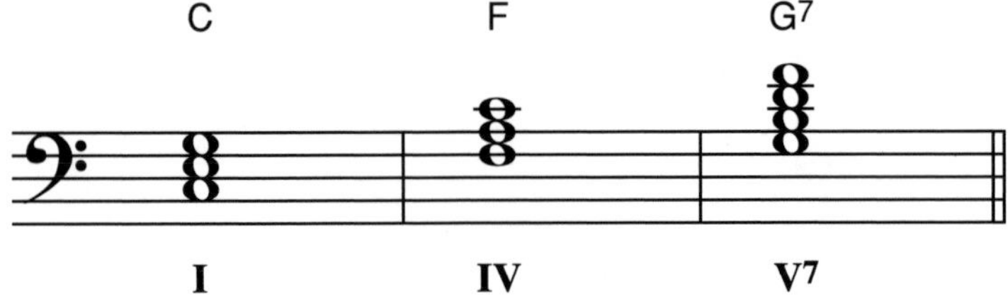

- **STEP 2:**

  THE C BLUES PROGRESSION (THE LEFT HAND CHORD PATTERN)

  A *blues progression* (pattern) is a series of chords which is usually 12 bars (measures) long. There are many variations, but a traditional blues progression generally consists of the **I** chord (four measures), **IV** chord (two measures), **I** chord (two measures), **V**^{7} chord (one measure), **IV** chord (one measure), and the **I** chord (two measures).

The C Major Blues Progression

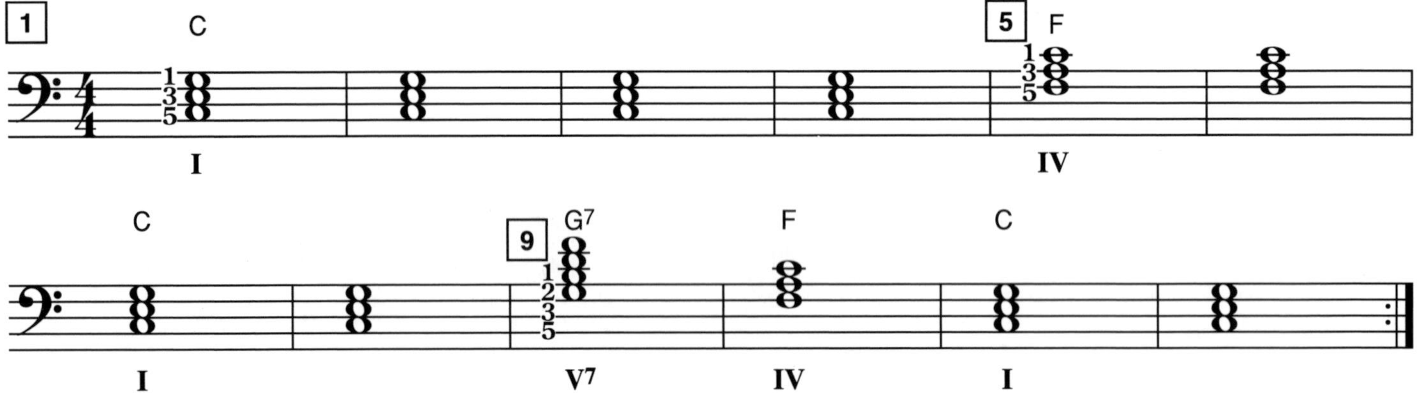

- **STEP 3:**

  THE C 5-FINGER BLUES SCALE (CREATING A MELODY)

  The C 5-finger Blues Scale has its own special sound.

  Practice this example for the right and left hands.

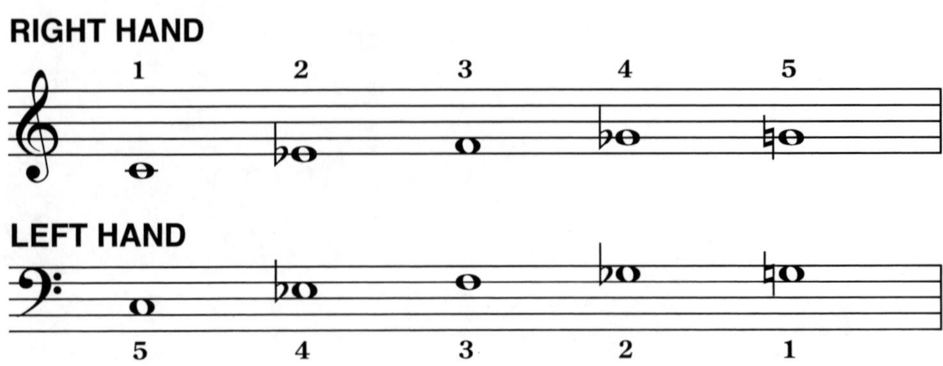

Alfred's

Teach Yourself To Play Blues

at the Keyboard

Everything you need to know to start playing the Blues now!

- For acoustic piano and electronic keyboard
- Teaches basic techniques & Blues scales
- Shows you how to play boogie bass
- Easy-to-follow instructions make learning fun

DR. BERT KONOWITZ
Professor of Music
Teachers College, Columbia University

Other Books in This Series

Teach Yourself Chords & Progressions (#17239)

Teach Yourself to Improvise (#16631)

Teach Yourself to Play Jazz (#17237)

Teach Yourself to Play Like a Pro (#17875)

Copyright © MCMXCVI by Alfred Publishing Co., Inc.
All rights reserved. Printed in USA.

Managing Editor: Morty Manus
Book Design: Susan Hartman

Cover Photography: Michael Lewellyn
Cover Design: Martha Widman/Ted Engelbart

...RD

Teach Yourself to Play Blues will have you playing the authentic sounds of the blues right from the beginning. By following the step-by-step set of instructions, you will learn all about blue notes, blues scales, blues progressions, grace notes and tremolos. This will prepare you to perform as a soloist or in a band.

Through the years, the blues style has stood as a basic thread around which jazz and rock have developed. As a result of the evolution of jazz and rock, the blues has taken on many different meanings for different people. To some, it is a specific type of chord progression in which blues singers offer musical messages of deep personal feelings, mostly dealing with love, jealousy, sadness and despair. The same blues chord progression also serves as the starting point from which instrumentalists create improvised melodies or written-out composition. Others propose that the blues is a mood, a style of performance, a state of mind.

Perhaps the beauty of the blues is that it is a musical experience through which all people—skilled musicians or untrained music lovers—can make or find a personal statement. Whether performed slow or fast, sad or happy, with words or without, by a soloist or a large musical group, the blues continues to survive many years of musical change because it touches something very basic in each of us.

Born out of the roots of slavery in America, the blues has since been performed worldwide. The true bedrock of the most influential blues is found in the Mississippi Delta. Later, as the blues merged with European musical forms, performers, ranging from solo guitarists with no formal musical training to blues singers performing with sophisticated backup bands, used the musical elements of the blues to create a wealth of musical repertoire.

From the last part of the 19th century, through the periods of World War I, the Depression of the '20s and '30s, the World War II era of the '40s and right up to today, the great names of jazz and rock have created and performed the blues. An all-star list would include Big Bill Broonzy, Leadbelly, Ma Rainey and Bessie Smith, Albert King, W. C. Handy, Louie Armstrong, Chuck Berry, Ray Charles, Elvis Presley, Muddy Waters, B. B. King, Jimi Hendrix, Eric Clapton and Aretha Franklin. The creative works of Count Basie, Duke Ellington, Benny Goodman and other swing bands of the '30s and '40s; the eventual development of the styles of Charlie Parker and the beboppers; and John Coltrane and Wynton Marsalis, all reflect the techniques and feelings of the blues. Jazz, rock and pop music of today still contain many ingredients of the blues.

This book is written to be played on either an acoustic piano or an electronic keyboard. Chord symbols are included and will help guitar and bass players to "fake" a rhythm background. Those seeking more specific bass lines should read the written left hand of each piece. All this makes it possible for a band to perform many varied blues patterns and sounds. The chord dictionary on page 78 should be used as a reference to aid in the use of chords.

IMPORTANT! Although this is a Teach Yourself book, any student will find it easier with the help of a competent teacher. If you run into difficulties, a teacher is a must. If you find that you are making rapid progress on your own, you will certainly learn even more rapidly with professional assistance. Learning music *with* a teacher is always easier than *without* a teacher.

About the CD

The companion CD features examples of the pieces (indicated by a track number) with background arrangements. Turn the balance all the way to the left to hear just the piano part; turn the balance all the way to the right to hear just the arrangement, minus the piano part. Keep it in the center for a perfect combination of both!

- **STEP 4:**

  PLAYING THE BLUES

  Now a melody created from the **C blues scale** is added to the **C blues progression** and …
  you are playing the blues!

Chasing the Blues Away

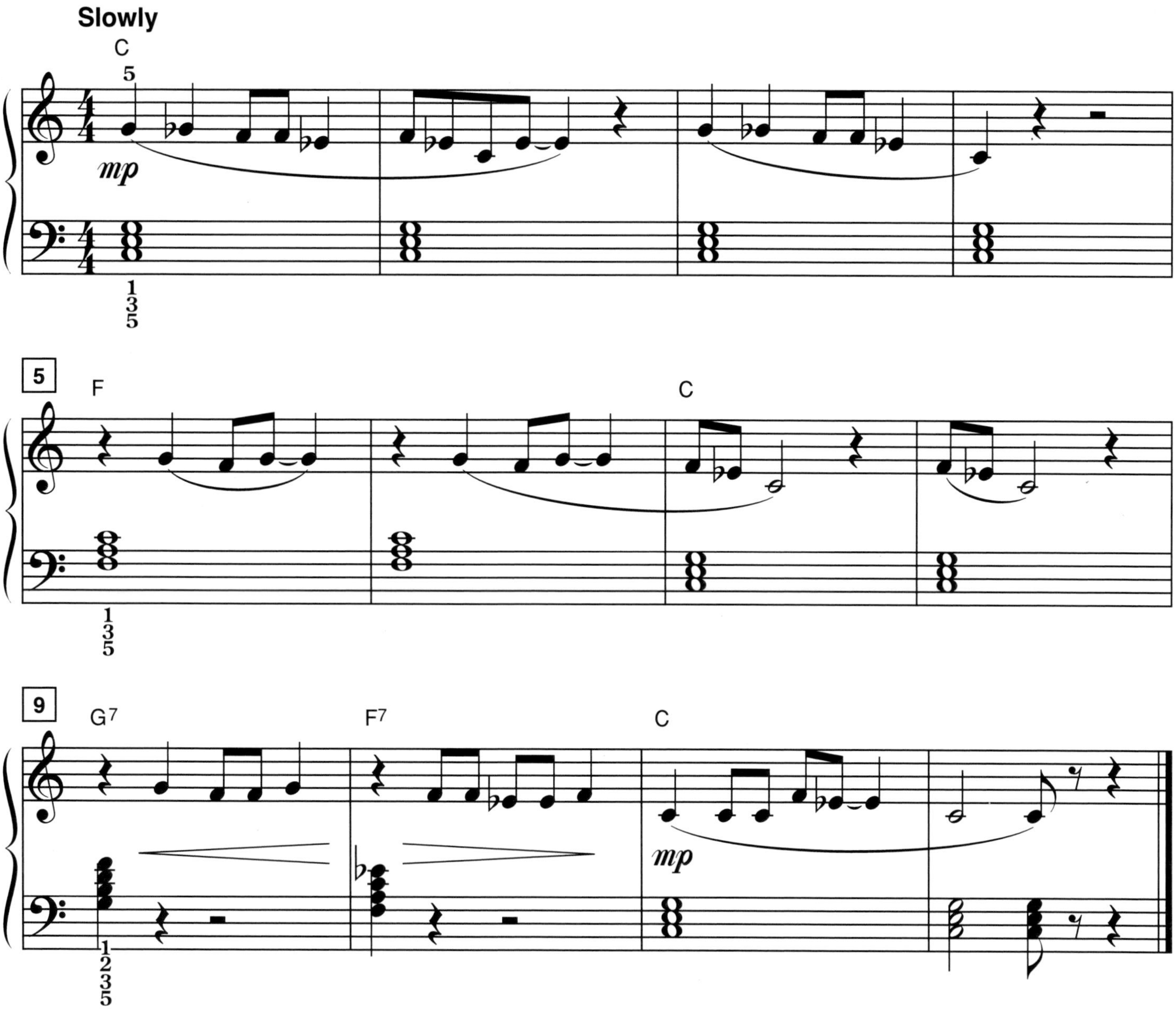

Slowly

C *mp* F C G7 F7 C *mp*

The **blues** is music for and about people. By using the special sounds of the **blues scale** and often using the 12-bar **blues chord progression,** the blues offers a way to express common feelings…sadness, loneliness, neglect, or even hope. Playing the **blues** helps you to express *your* feelings in a musical way that is satisfying because it makes *you* feel better.

* See "About the CD" section on page 4.

Playing (and Singing) the Blues

This **blues progression** helps to deliver an important message. Keep the blues tradition and sing as you perform. Notice the slight variation of the blues progression in measure 2 (F chord). It's done often.

It's the Little Things That Count the Most Blues

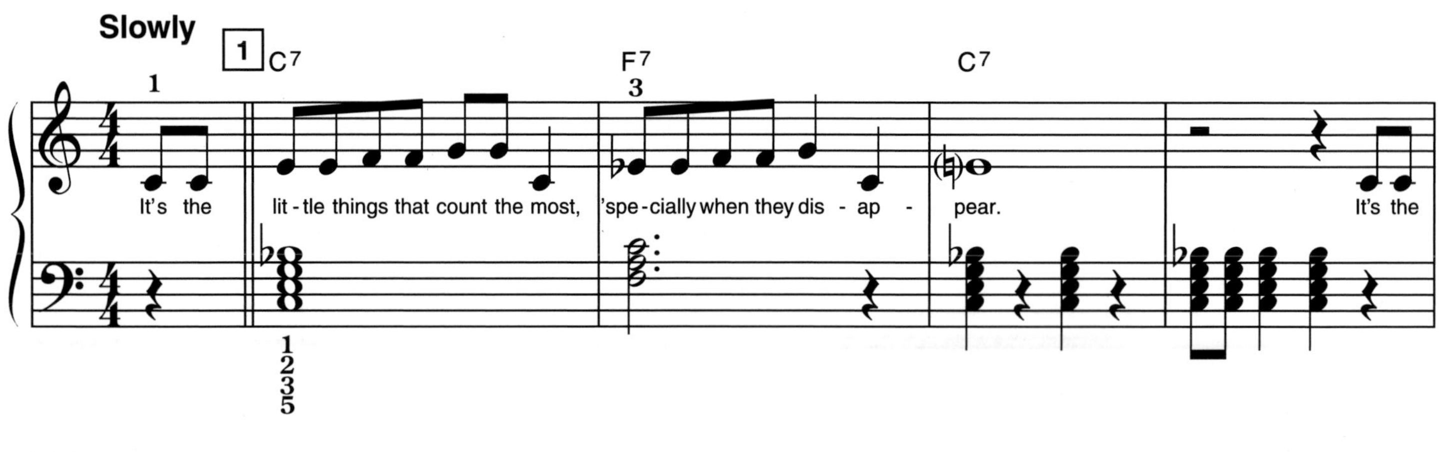

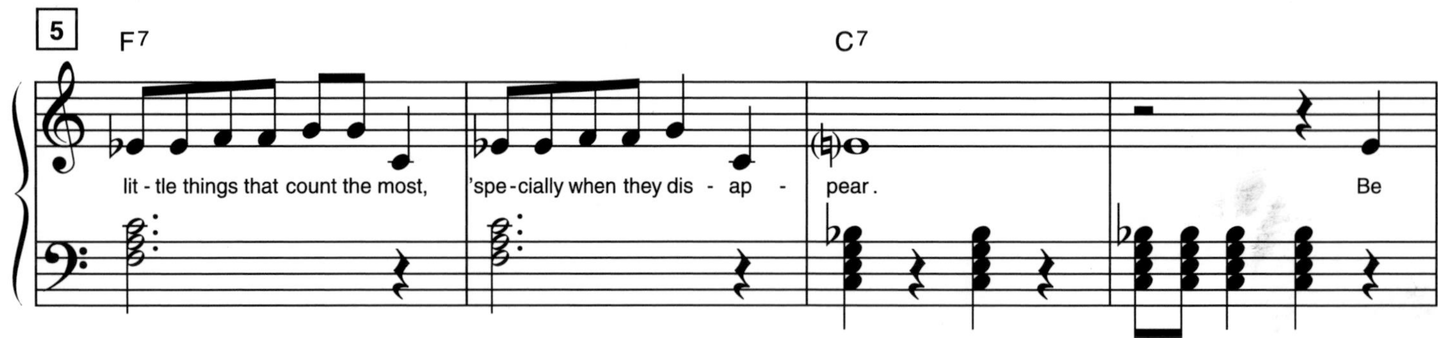

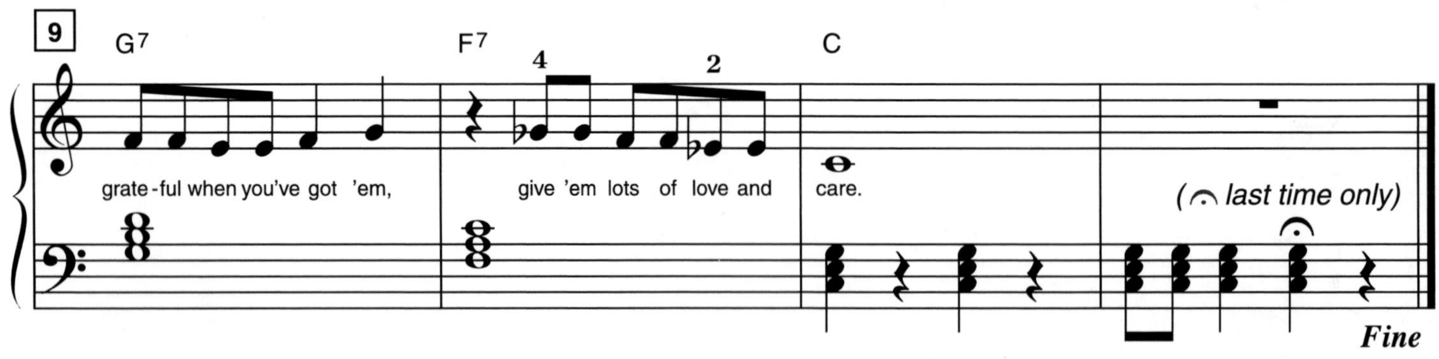

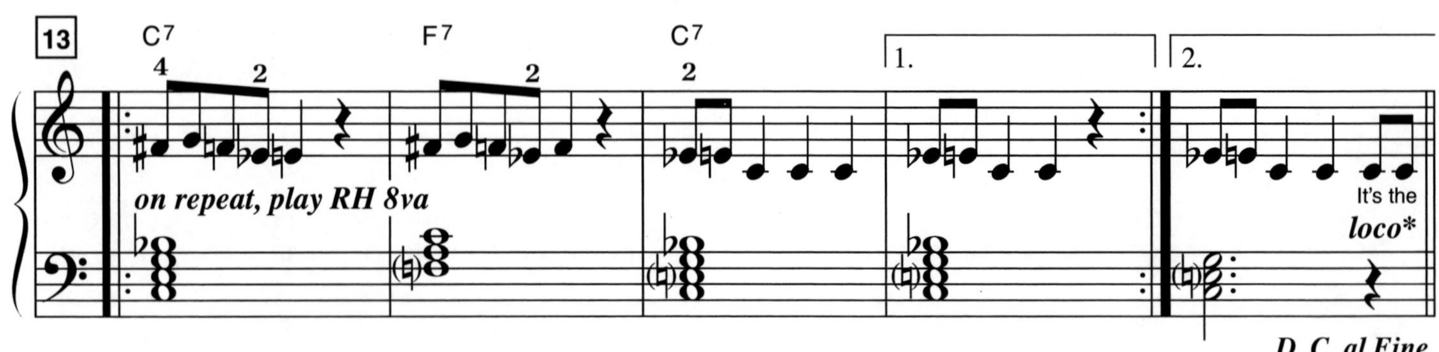

**Loco* means to play "as written." (In this case, *not* an octave higher.)

CHORD TONES AND JAZZ ACCENTS

The individual tones that make up a chord are called **chord tones.** They may be used to create new melodies. See measure 5 for the C chord tones, measure 9 for the F chord tones and measure 13 for the G chord tones. Now, swing these chord tones by playing accents on the 2nd and 4th beats when indicated.

The Swing Parade Blues

March tempo

C G C

mf *Fine*

5 C7

9 F7 C7

13 G7 F7 C7 C

D. C. al Fine

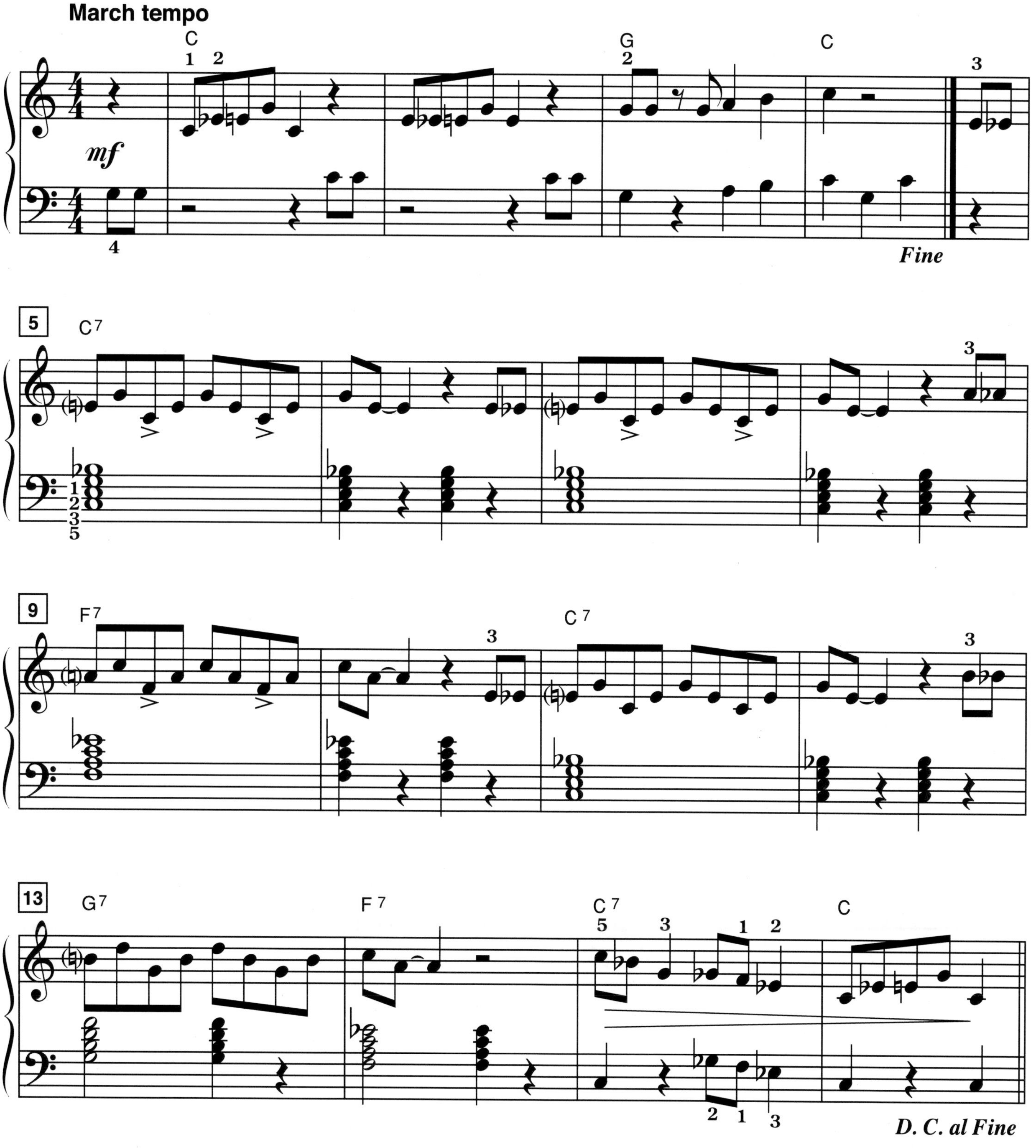

Three Easy Steps to Teach Yourself to Add a Left-Hand Rhythm Bass

- **Step 1:**

THE WALKING BASS

The **walking bass** is a left-hand pattern that is used in the Blues to create a rhythm background. Practice each one several times. (Observe the accent signs to give it that authentic blues sound.)

- **Step 2:**

THE WALKING BASS WITH VARIED RHYTHMS

Walkin' on Down

* Play *mp* the first time, *mf* on the repeat.

** Fingering in **(1)** means play **1** on the repeat.

• **Step 3:**
THE WALKING BASS PLAYS THE BLUES PROGRESSION

BLUES ACCENTS

From this point on, accent the 2nd and 4th beats of each measure whenever possible.

Bass Beat Blues

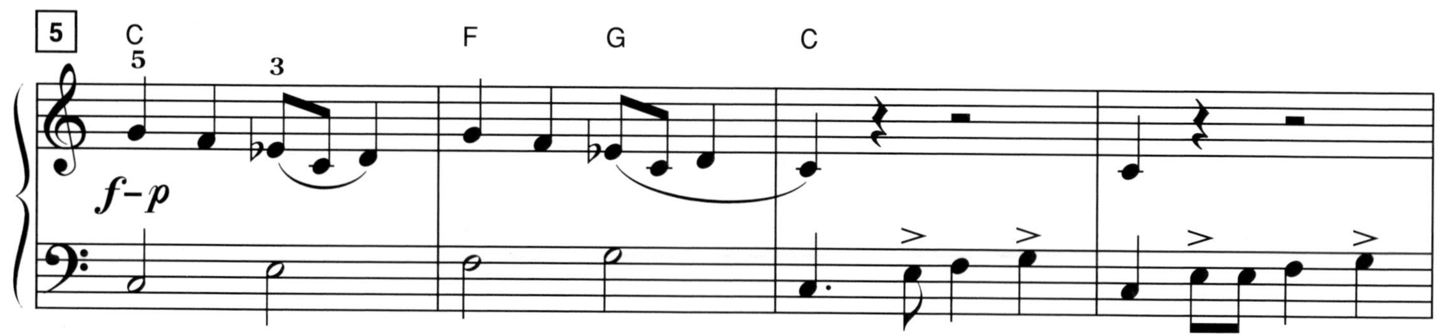

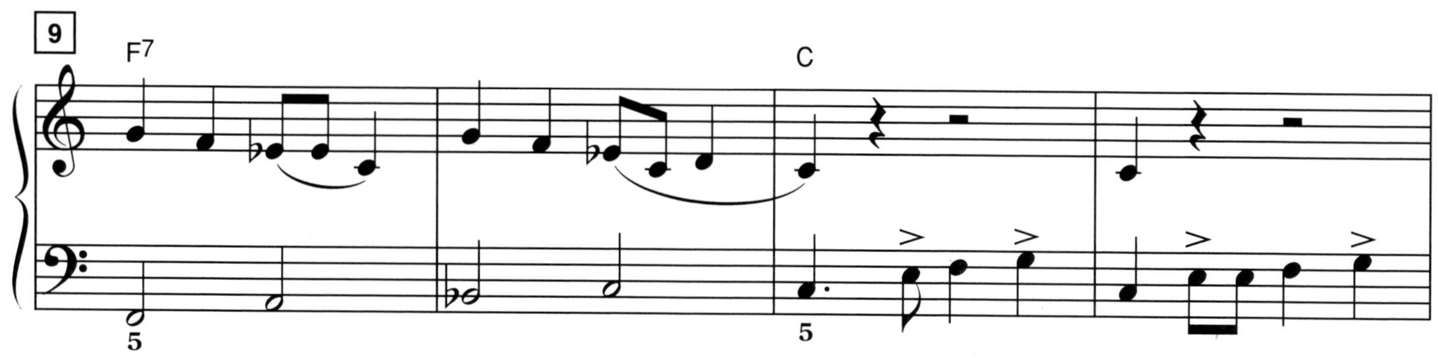

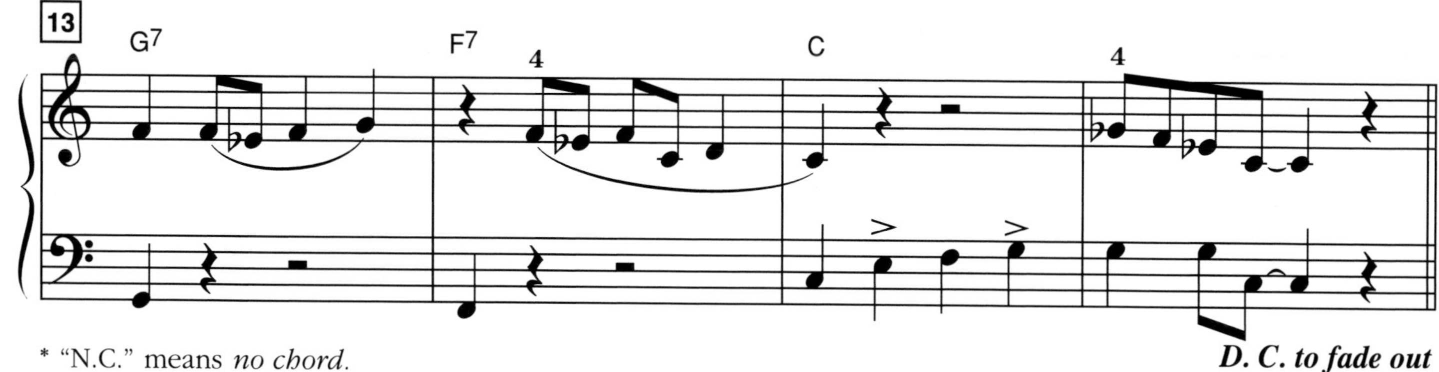

* "N.C." means *no chord.*

Blues Jam: The Walking Bass

Walking with the Count

Count Basie was an exciting Jazz pianist and band leader. He and his band often used this version of the walking bass as a rhythm background. Check out his inspirational style on CDs and tapes.

Easy, walking tempo

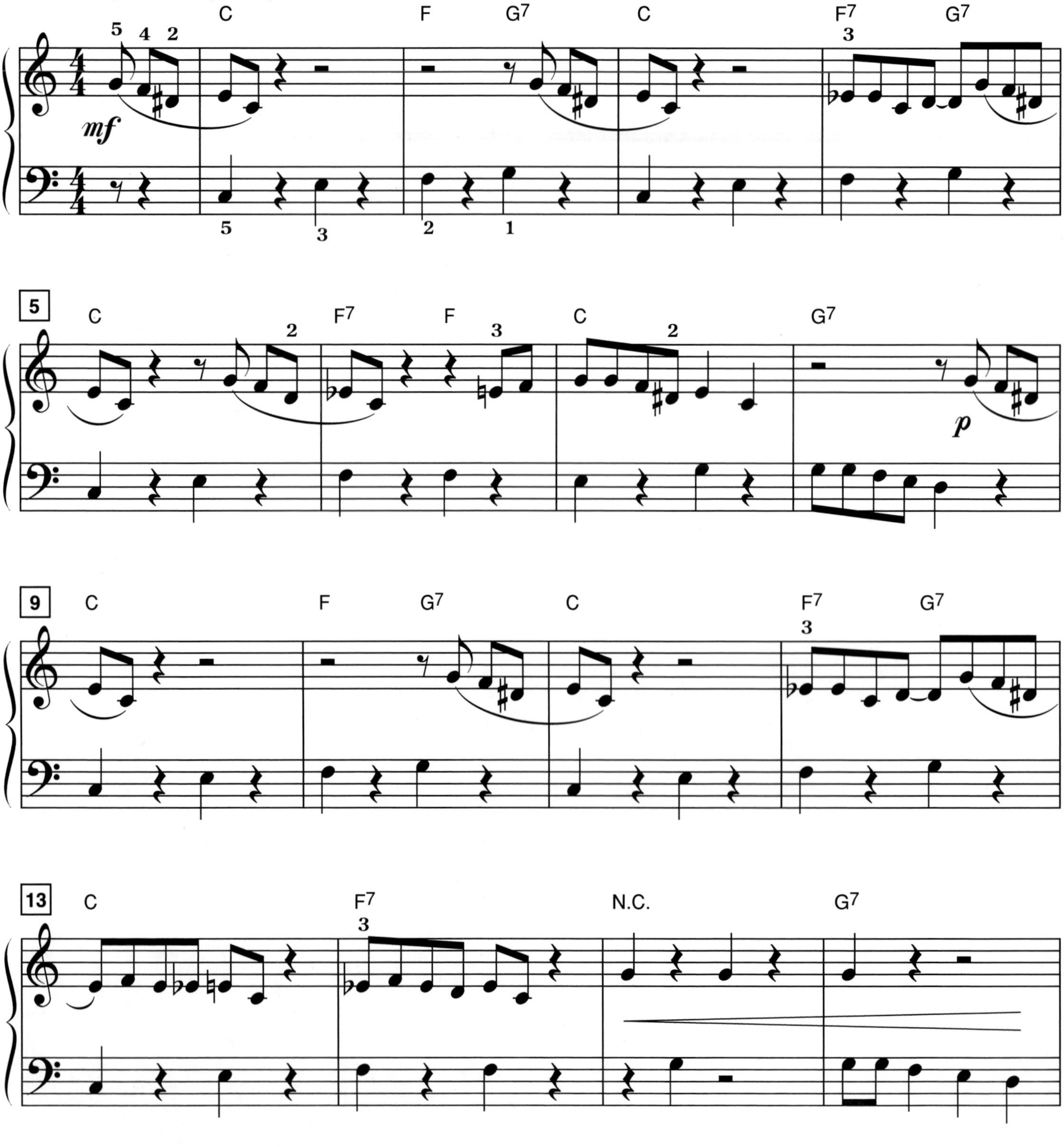

C F G7 C F7 G7

5 C F7 F C G7

9 C F G7 C F7 G7

13 C F7 N.C. G7

* This is the "Basie ending," which "The Count" created to end many of his pieces.

Blue Notes Create New Melodies

Blue notes (marked here with an "*") are flatted tones on the 3rd and 5th steps of the major scale that often return to their neighboring tone one half-step higher.

First Five Steps of a C Major Scale

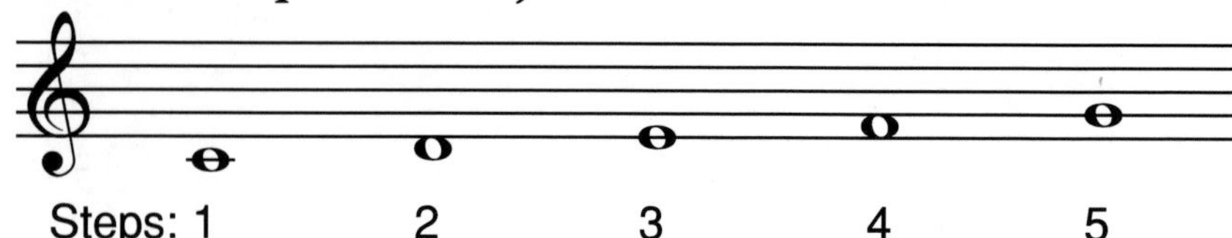

First Five Steps of a C Blues Scale

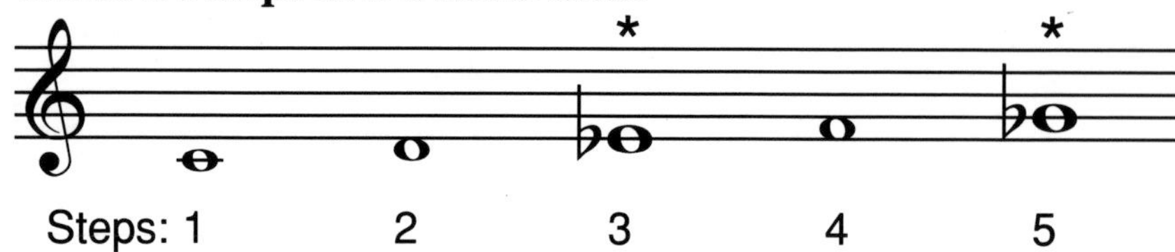

Play this example which does *not* use blue notes.

Now play this same example and hear the difference that the flatted 3rd and 5th blue notes (*) make.

Flatted Third Blue Notes

Flatted Fifth Blue Notes

Blue Notes Performance Piece

The blues progression can be played in a slow and easy manner. Warm up by first playing measures 1–4 several times with the LH alone, then play the whole piece.

Practice these bass rhythms which use blue notes to create the Blues sound. Don't forget to accent the left hand on the 2nd and 4th beats whenever possible.

The Walking Blue Note Bass

Blues for Wynton Marsalis

Wynton Marsalis, a great jazz trumpet player, grew up in New Orleans, a city known for great blues. Wynton plays the blues with jazz groups, as well as classical music with the world's finest symphony orchestras.

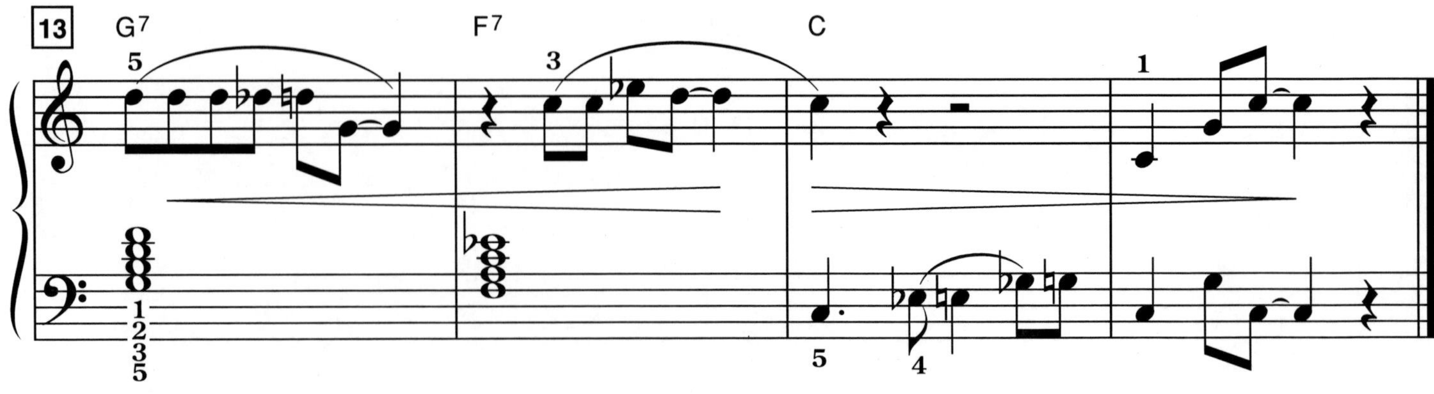

Walking Blue Note Performance Piece

Early Morning Blues

Practice each **Walking Blue Note Bass** slowly before playing Early Morning Blues.

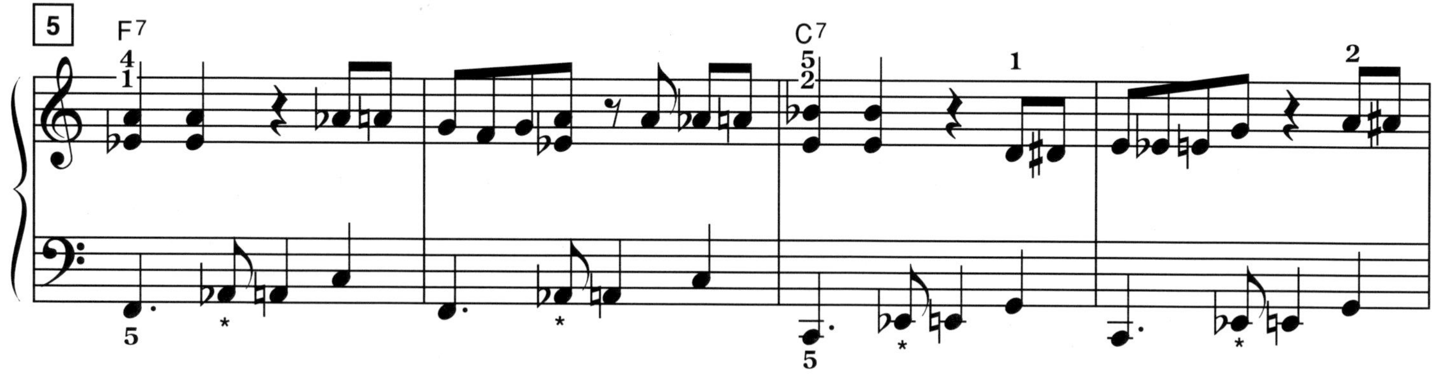

* Blue notes are marked with an *.

Blue Note Walking Bass and Accents

Getting It Right from the Start

The unique blues sound is created by using a number of different techniques, including the **blue note walking bass** (measure 3, LH), **accents** played on the 2nd and 4th beats (measure 5, LH), **blues scales** (measure 5, RH) and **blue notes** (measure 9, RH). You can't lose with this combination!

Moderato

C F C7 F C

mf

5 F7 C

9 G7 C

13 C F7 C F7

Play 2 times, changing the dynamics each time (p or f), then go on.

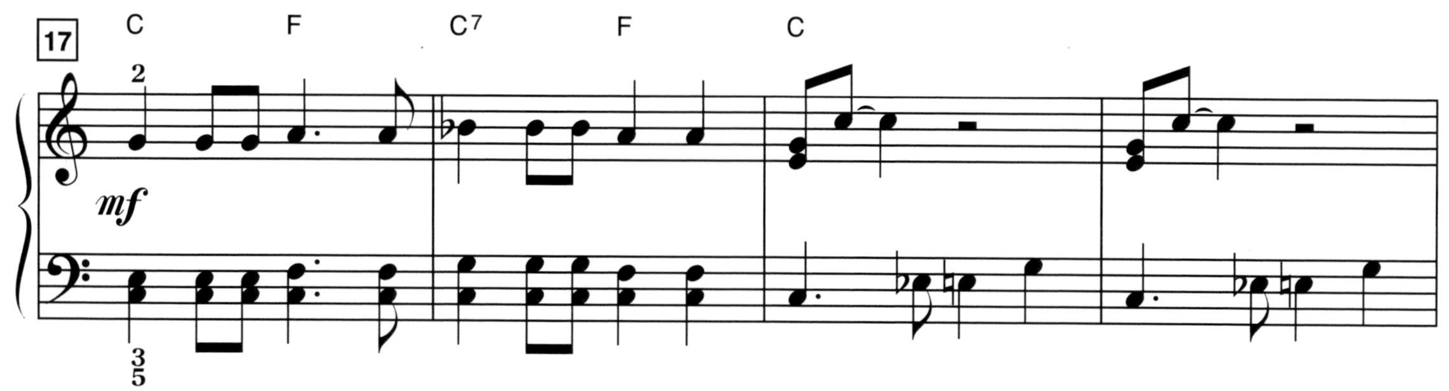

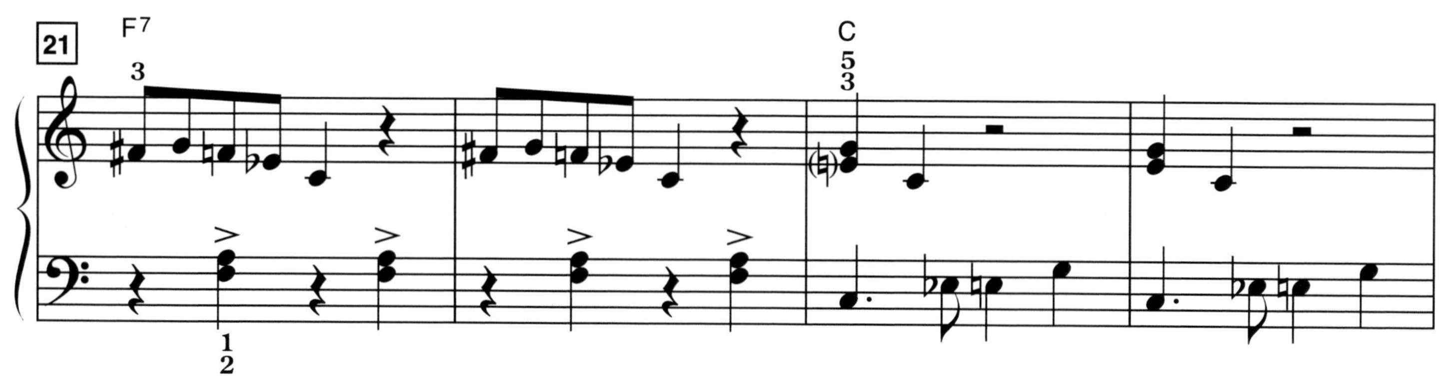

* *sfz* means "with a strong accent."

The Complete C Blues Scale

The unique blues sound is created by using the tones of the full blues scale. Learn and memorize the tones of the full **C Blues Scale** by practicing each hand separately in both ascending and descending order.

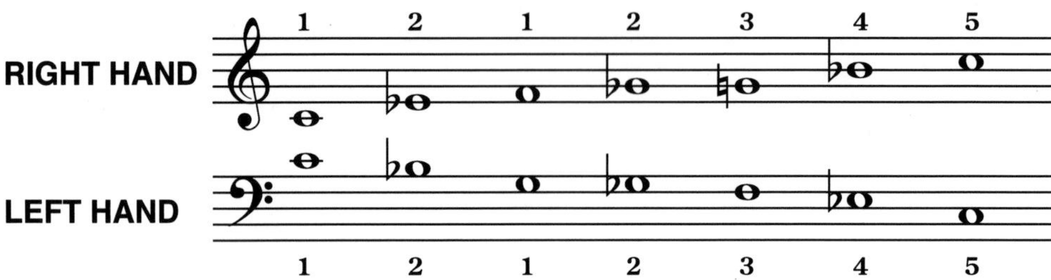

Meet the Flatted 7th

Important! There are three Blue Notes (*) in the Complete C Blues Scale: E♭ (flatted 3rd), G♭ (flatted 5th) and B♭ (flatted 7th).

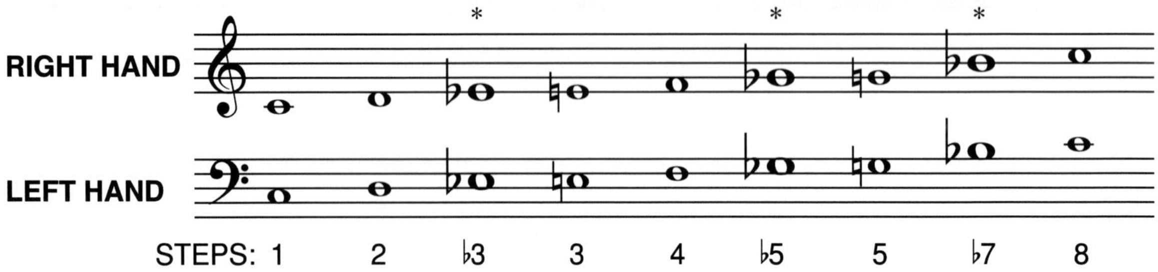

Blue Sounds

Practice the left hand in measure 1 several times before performing.

1st time, play the entire piece using *Rock-style* (even) eighth notes in the right hand:
2nd time, play the entire piece using *Jazz-style* (slightly uneven) eighth notes in the right hand:

C Blues Scale Performance Piece

Get Up and Go Blues

The **C blues scale** is used here to create a swingin' Blues chart. Many Blues charts heard on CDs, radio and TV use the Blues Scale in similar ways.

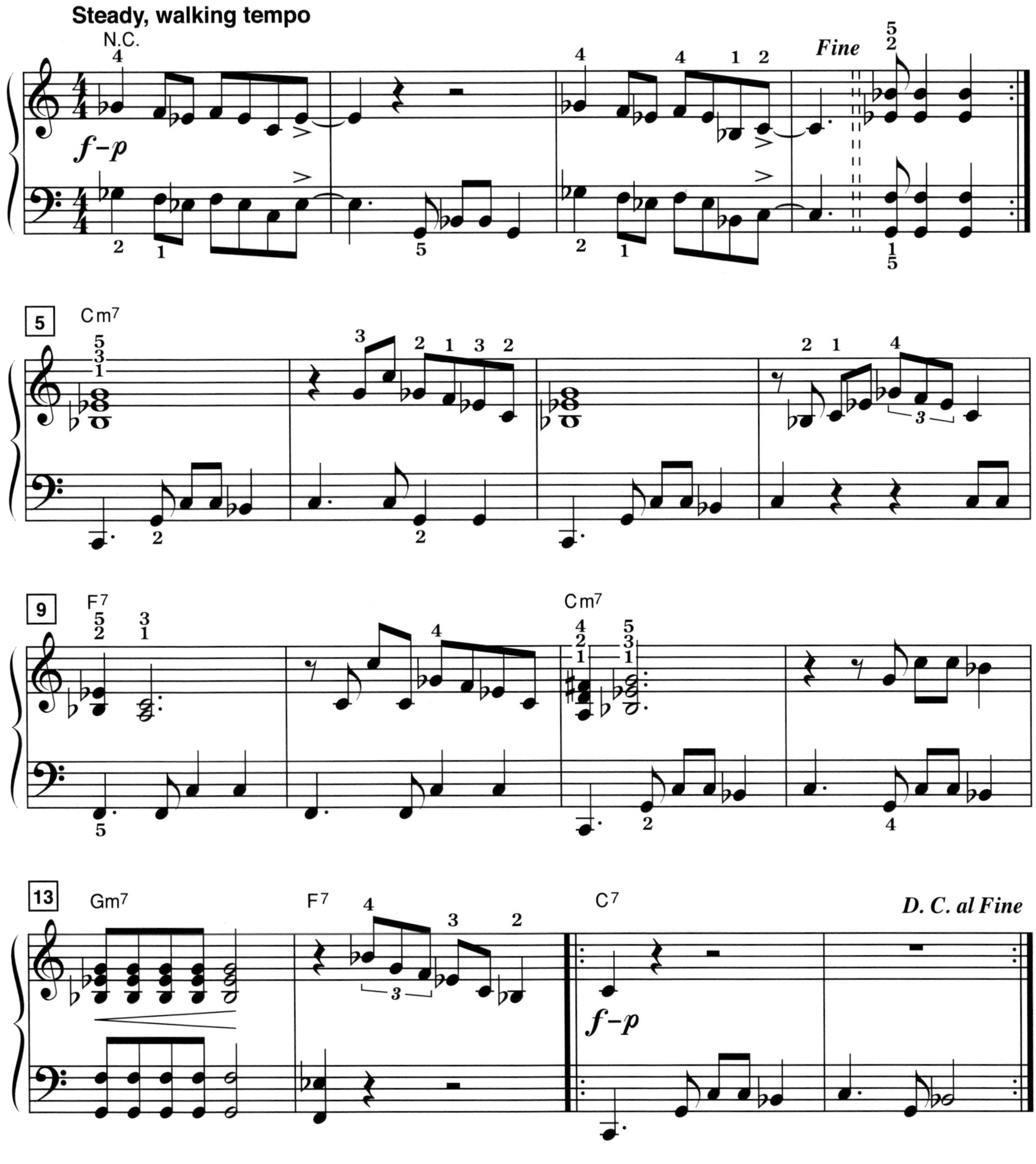

Steady, walking tempo

N.C. *f–p* *Fine*

5 Cm7

9 F7 Cm7

13 Gm7 F7 C7 *D. C. al Fine* *f–p*

Boogie Left Hand

Comin' On Home Boogie

This familiar-sounding left-hand **boogie** pattern is one of many that are heard in Blues music. In this piece, the left hand builds a strong rhythmic background.

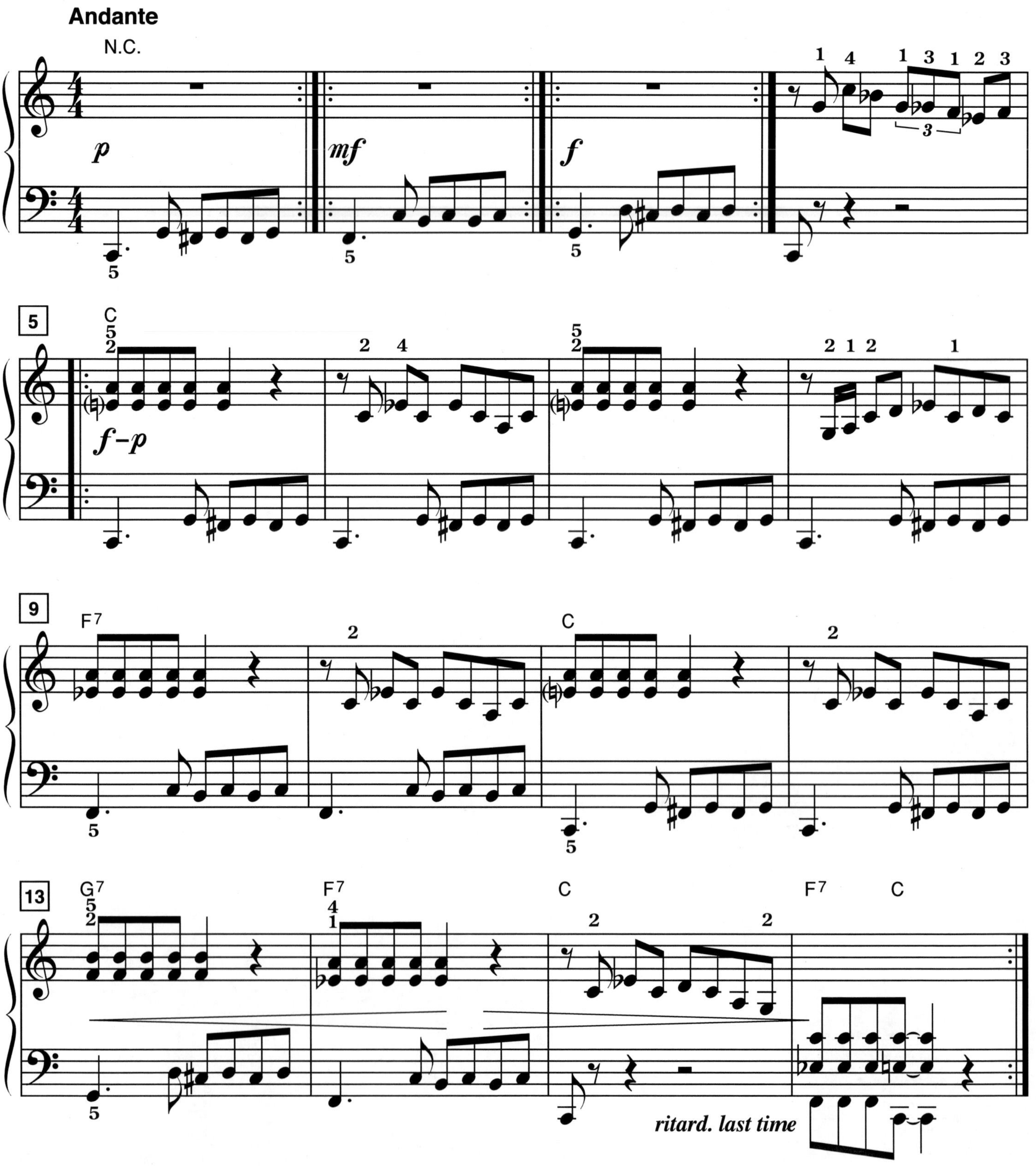

Andante

N.C.

C

F7 C

G7 F7 C F7 C

ritard. last time

Boogie Performance Piece

Sleepy Town Boogie

Blues players often use **boogie patterns** at a *slow tempo* to create a haunting, melancholy mood. The triplet figure intro comes out of the Rhythm and Blues style.

Slow rock tempo

C, C7, N.C., F7, Fm, C, G7, F7, C, N.C., C, C7, D♭7, C7

mp–mf

mf–f

ritard.

5, 9, 13, 17

RUBATO INTRO

Rubato means to play freely, slightly slowing down or speeding up the tempo. Take plenty of time to play the rubato introduction. Then get right into this blues swinger, using a combination left-hand **walking blue note** and **boogie bass.**

Whenever You're Ready Blues

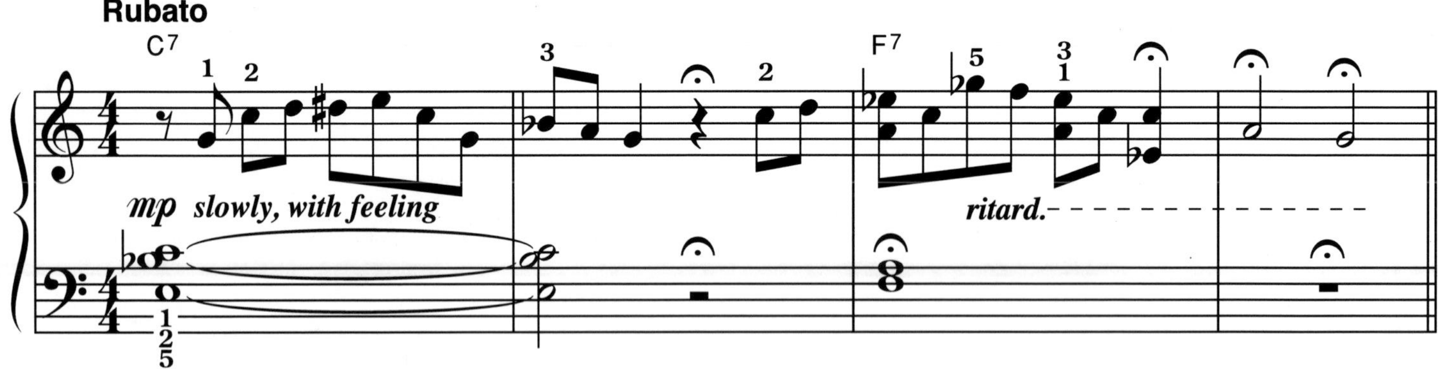

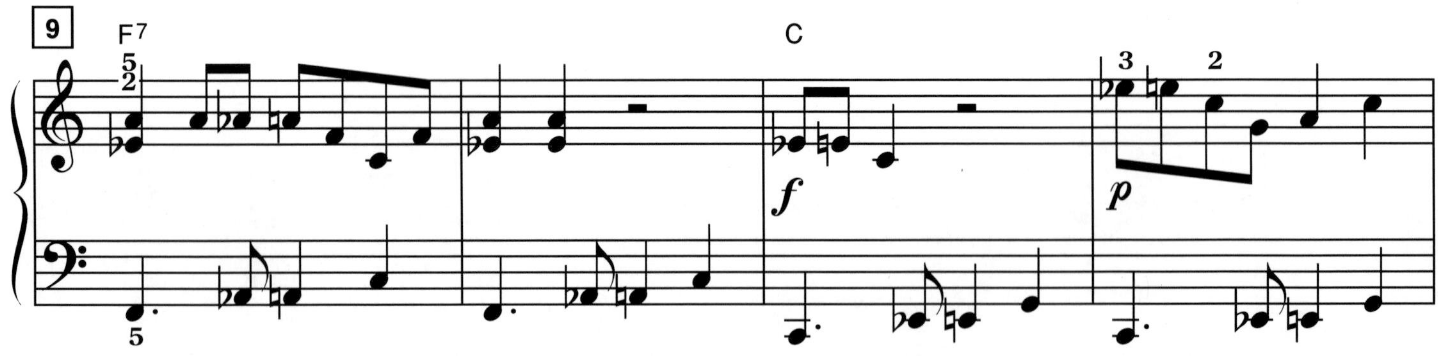

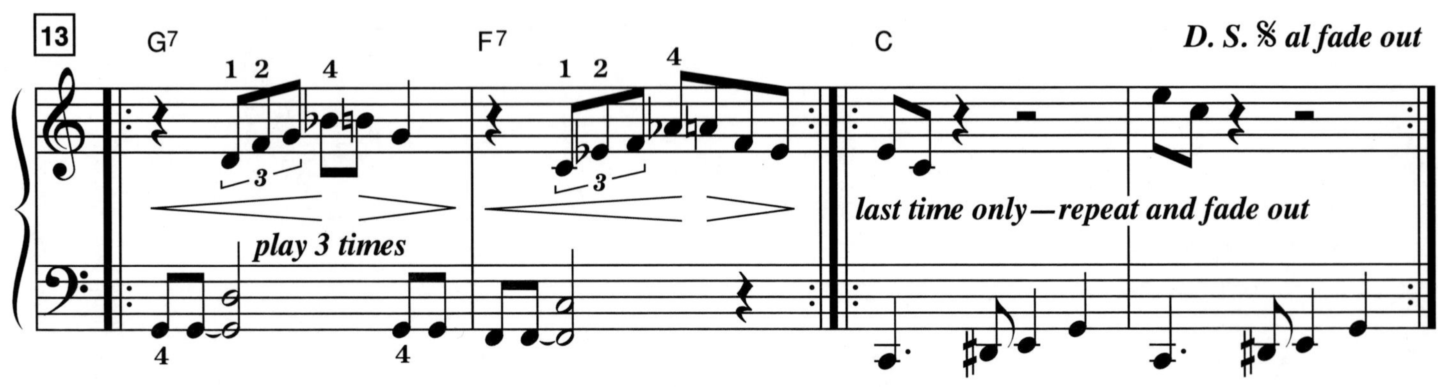

Eight-to-the-Bar Boogie

Eight-to-the-Bar Boogie Blues

This great-sounding Boogie bass pattern is often called "eight-to-the-bar," because it uses eight eighth notes in a measure. Warm up by first playing measures 1–4 several times with the LH alone, then play in a blues style.

Easy, relaxed tempo

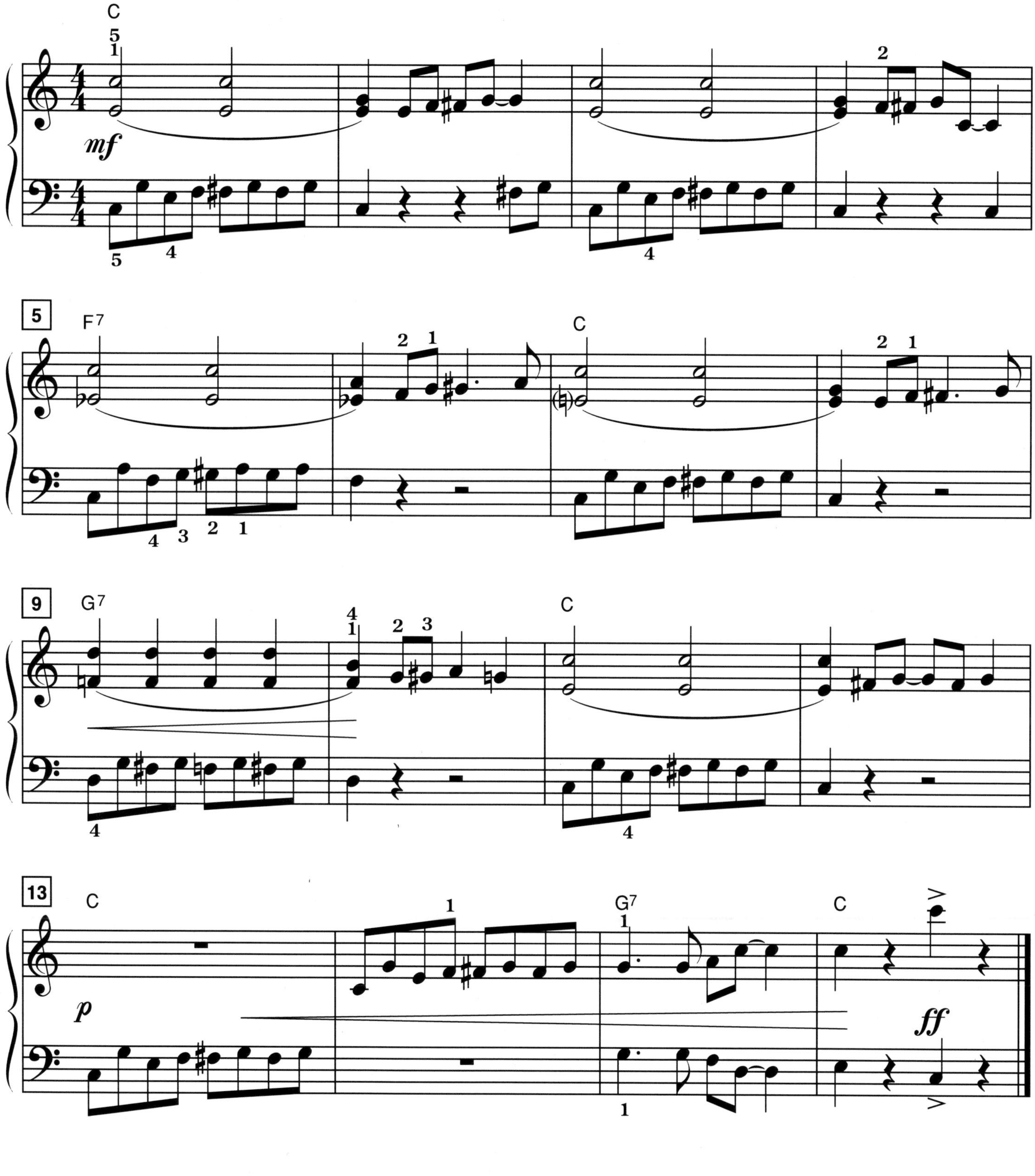

C mf

5 F7 C

9 G7 C

13 C p G7 C ff

Warm up by first practicing this famous left hand boogie pattern—then notice how the sound of the blues comes alive when a melody with lots of blue notes is added.

West Wind Boogie

Moderato

C7

mp–mf

4

F7

7

C7

G

10

F

C

F7

C

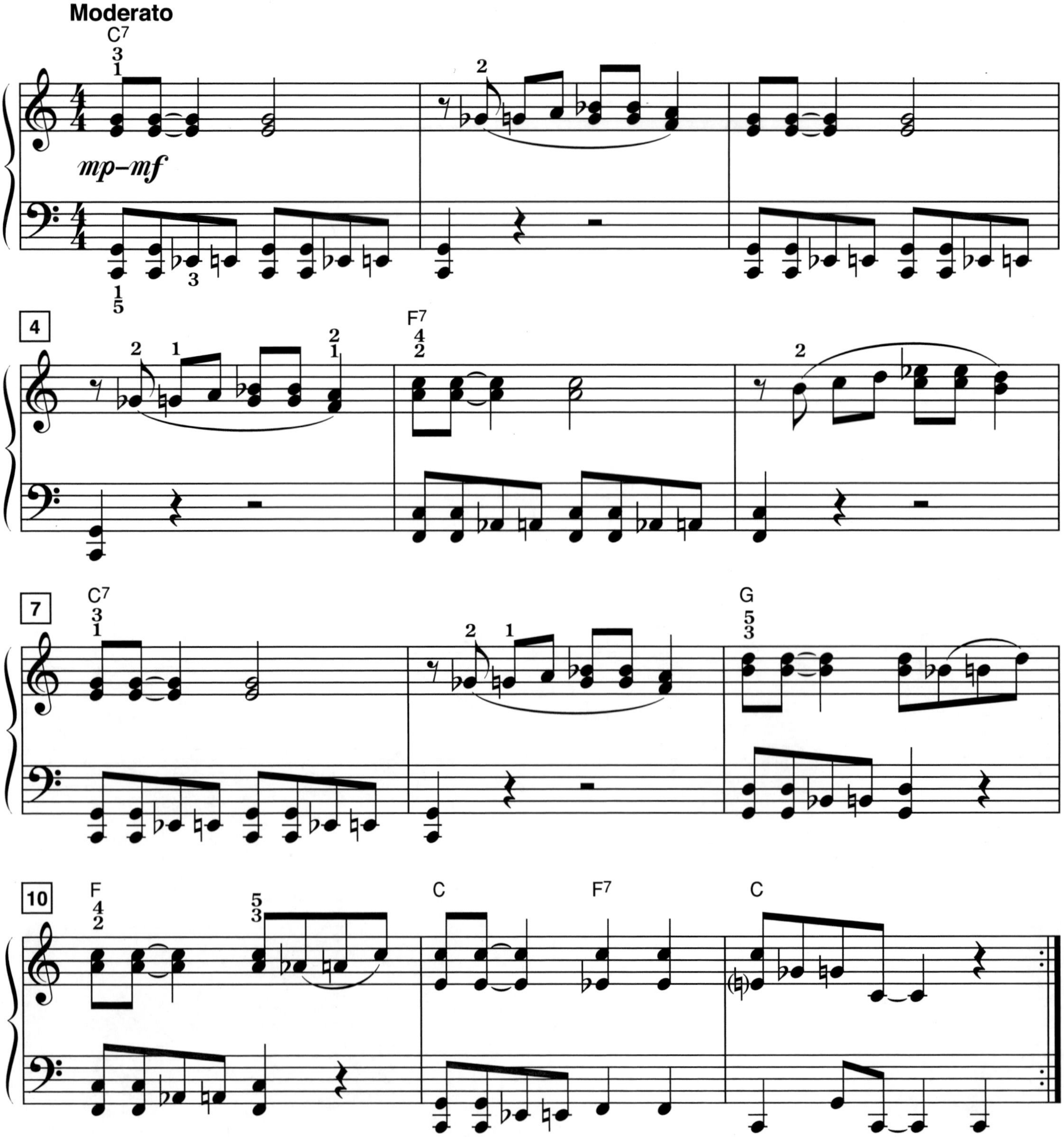

Rubato Intro and Double-Note Boogie

Blues for the Piano Player

Take your time on every note in the **rubato intro.** Then get that left hand choppin' away at this hot **double-note boogie bass.**

Track 16

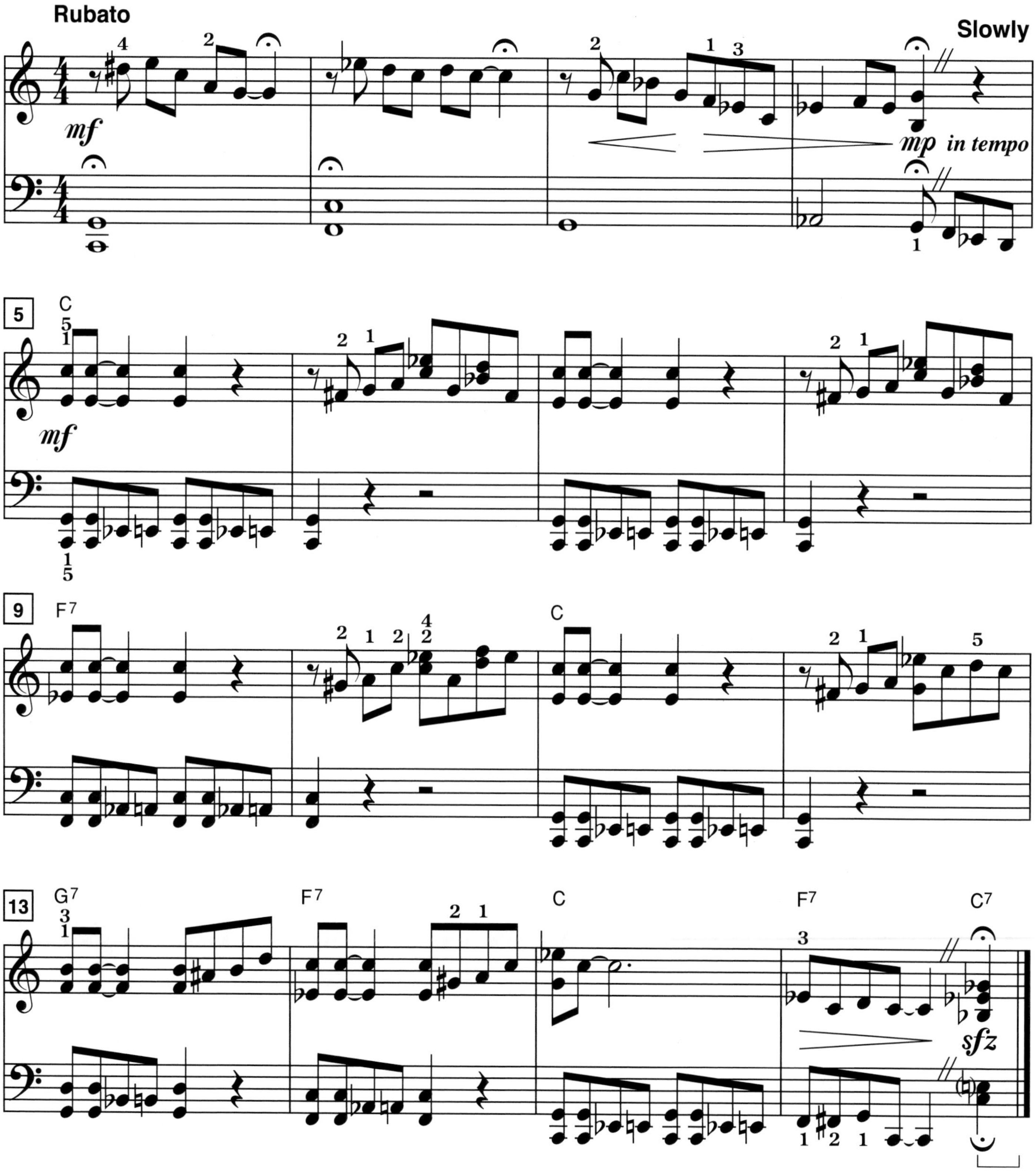

Rubato
Slowly
mf
mp in tempo
5
C
mf
9
F7
C
13
G7
F7
C
F7
C7
sfz

Double-Note Boogie Performance Piece

Each tone in the left hand is played as a double note in this boogie bass. The **tremolo** (𝄚) on the last chord is played by alternating the fingers back and forth very quickly on the two indicated notes in each hand—then hold the last tone with the pedal.

Little Joe Boogie

Very slow

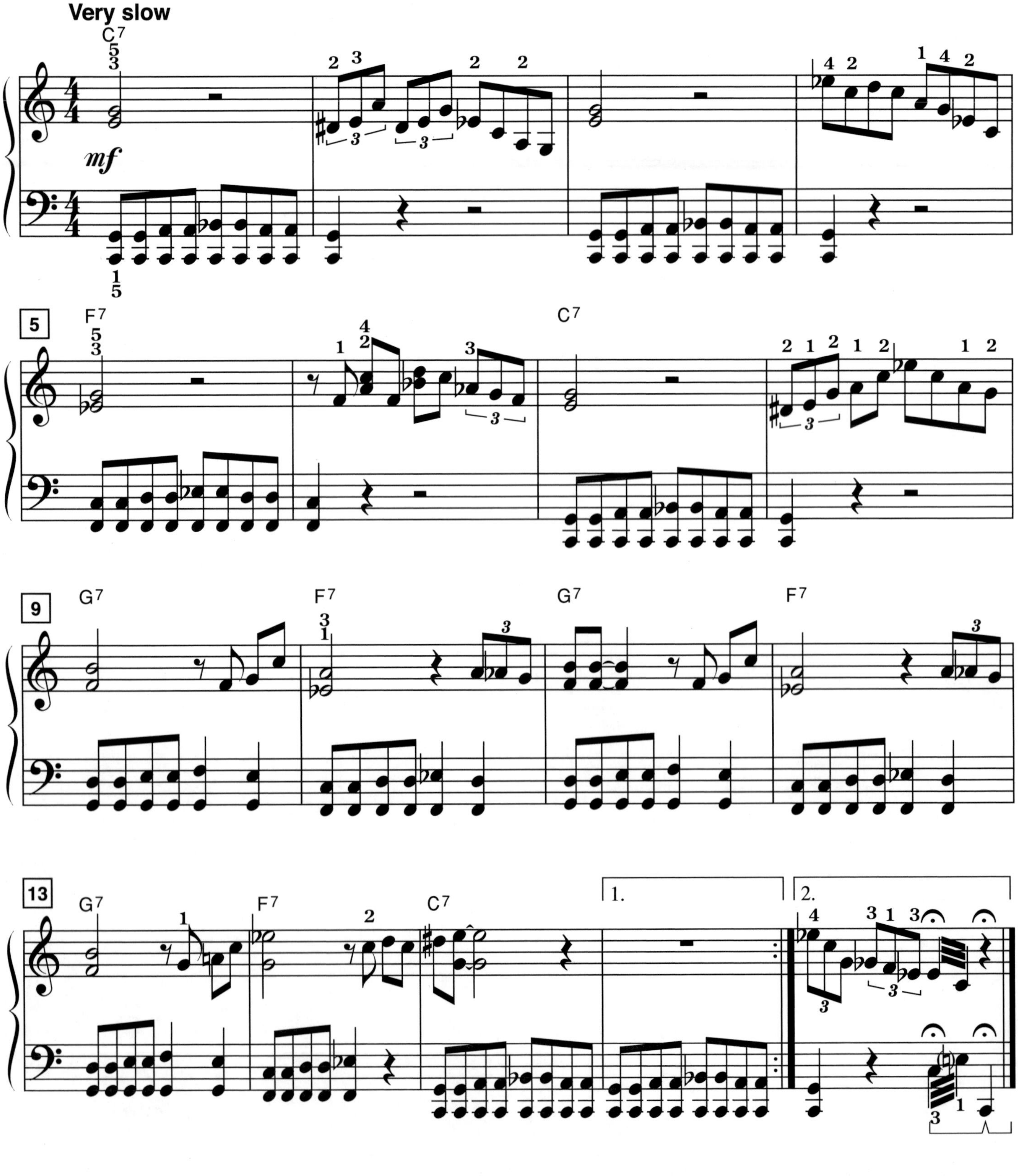

Track 18

Bugle Call Boogie

This **rolling boogie bass** (measures 5–9) helps to produce a Blues that will "bring down the house." If it doesn't, then play it again at a slightly faster tempo … that should do it!

March tempo (Jazz-style ♩♪)

Fine

mp

5 F7 C

f

9 Dm7 G C

13 Dm7 F7 A♭ C

mf *mp*

D. C. al Fine

Blues Jam

Track 19

Growing Pains Blues

Moderately slow (Jazz Style ♫)

Cm7

mp

5 F7 C7

mf

9 G7 F7 Cm7

13 C N.C.

17
F
C
21
G7
F7
C7
G7
25
C
F♯7
29
F7
C
33
G
G7
C
G
C7

C BLUES PROGRESSION & CHORD VOICINGS

Now that the 12-bar **blues progression** is "in your fingers," you are ready to learn how to play the basic blues chords in different positions. The three basic 7th chords used in the C blues progression are:

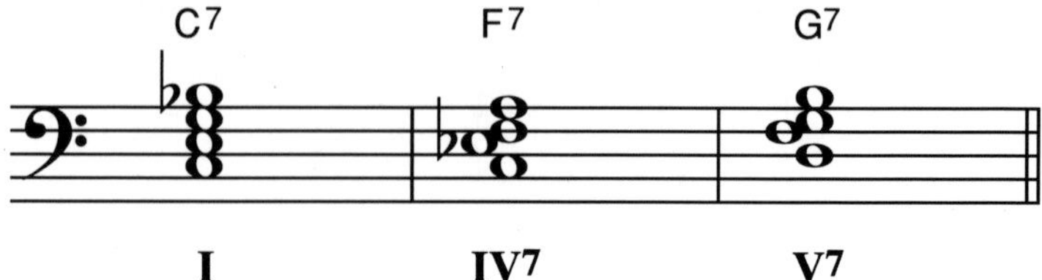

What is Full Chord Voicing? Full Chord Voicing is when you use all the notes of the chord. Playing full-voice chords from the root up (1st, 3rd, 5th, 7th) can create awkward fingering and clunky-sounding accompaniment. That's why Full Chord Voicings in chord progressions are often re-voiced, or re-arranged, for better-sounding and easier-fingering progressions.

Full Chord Voicing for C: The re-voicing of the F **(IV7)** and the G7 **(V7)** chords allow for smoother and easier movement between chords.*

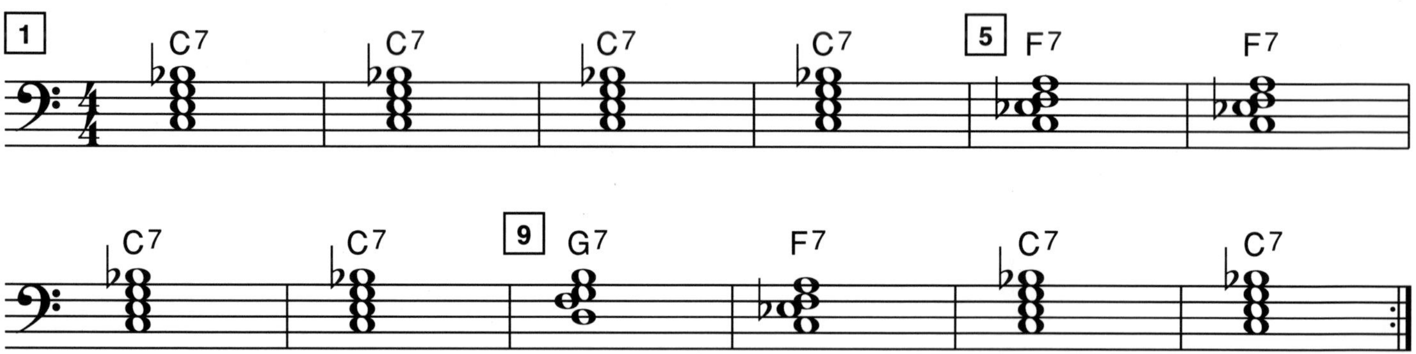

What is Interval Voicing? Interval voicing means to only play some of the notes of a chord rather than all of them. The purpose of interval voicing is to create variety and contrast by using a lighter and more open sound. Usually, only the 3rd and flatted ♭7th tones of the chords are played.

Interval Voicing for C: In this example, the interval voicing begins with the flatted 7th of the C7 chord in the bass with the 3rd above it. The voicings following it are selected to create the least amount of movement between tones.*

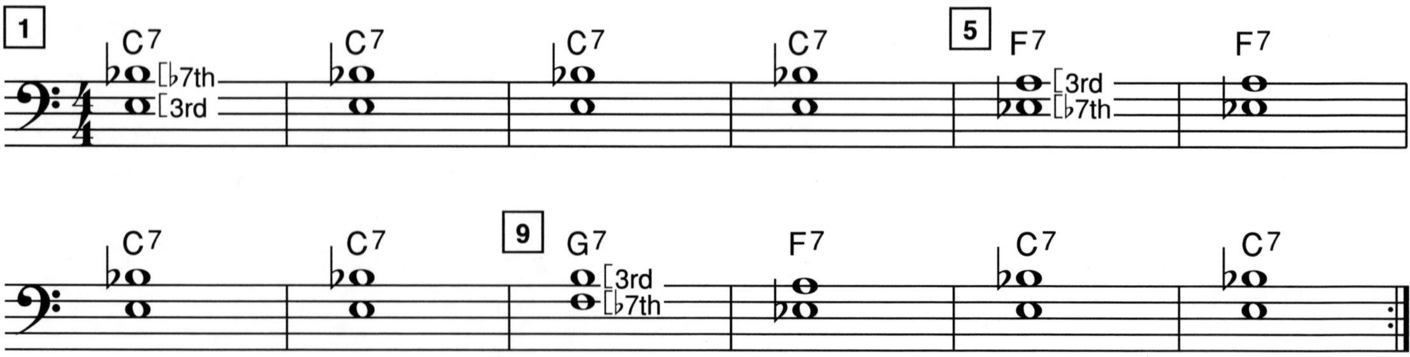

*Practice the full chord and interval voicings slowly until memorized.

C Blues Progression Performance Piece

Mountain Top Blues

Measures 1–12 demonstrate how **full chord voicings** and **interval voicings** are used in a 12-bar blues progression. This left hand is worth memorizing so that it can be used in other blues progression pieces.

Slowly

Walking Bass Line in "C"

You've been introduced to elements of the **walking bass line,** but here it is in its complete 12-bar quarter-note pattern. The **walking bass line** is an important left-hand technique that adds a strong rhythmic feeling. It's major characteristic is a tone played on *each* beat of *each* measure as it *outlines* the indicated chord.

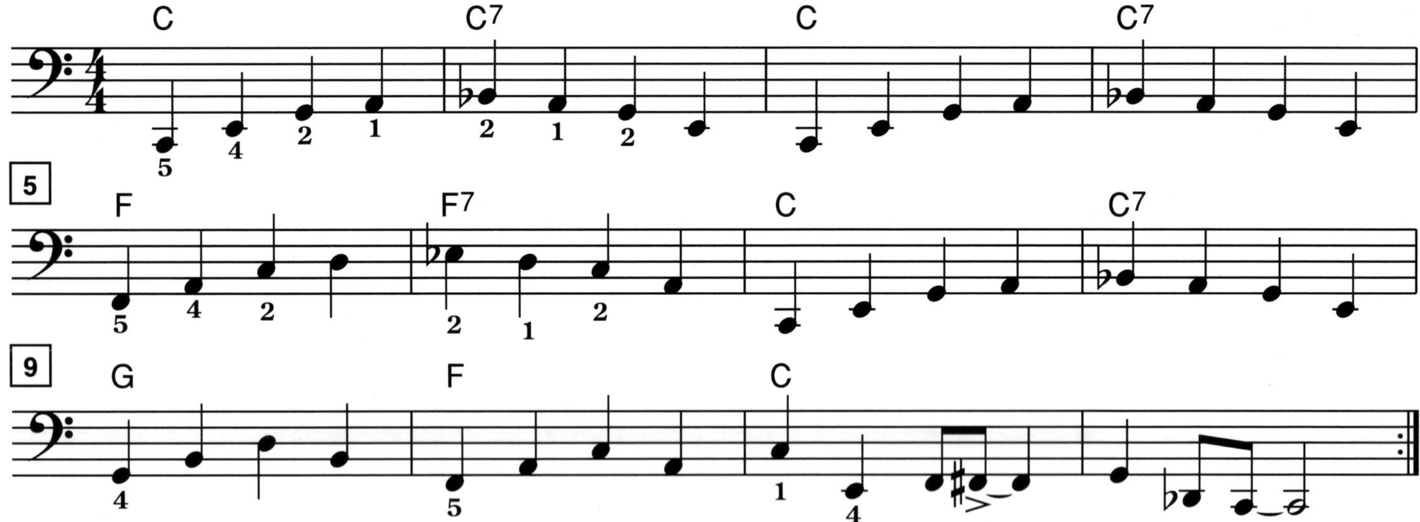

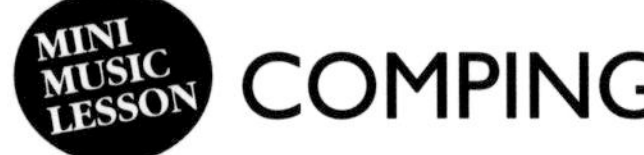

C C7 C C7
5 F F7 C C7
9 G F C

MINI MUSIC LESSON **COMPING** **Comping** is a rhythmic technique in which chords are performed in a short, punctuated manner as an accompaniment pattern. In **Walking Together Blues,** the comping chords add rhythmic punch to the left-hand walking bass line.

Walking Together Blues

Andante
C C7 C C7
mf–p
5 F7 C C7
9 G7 F7 C F G C

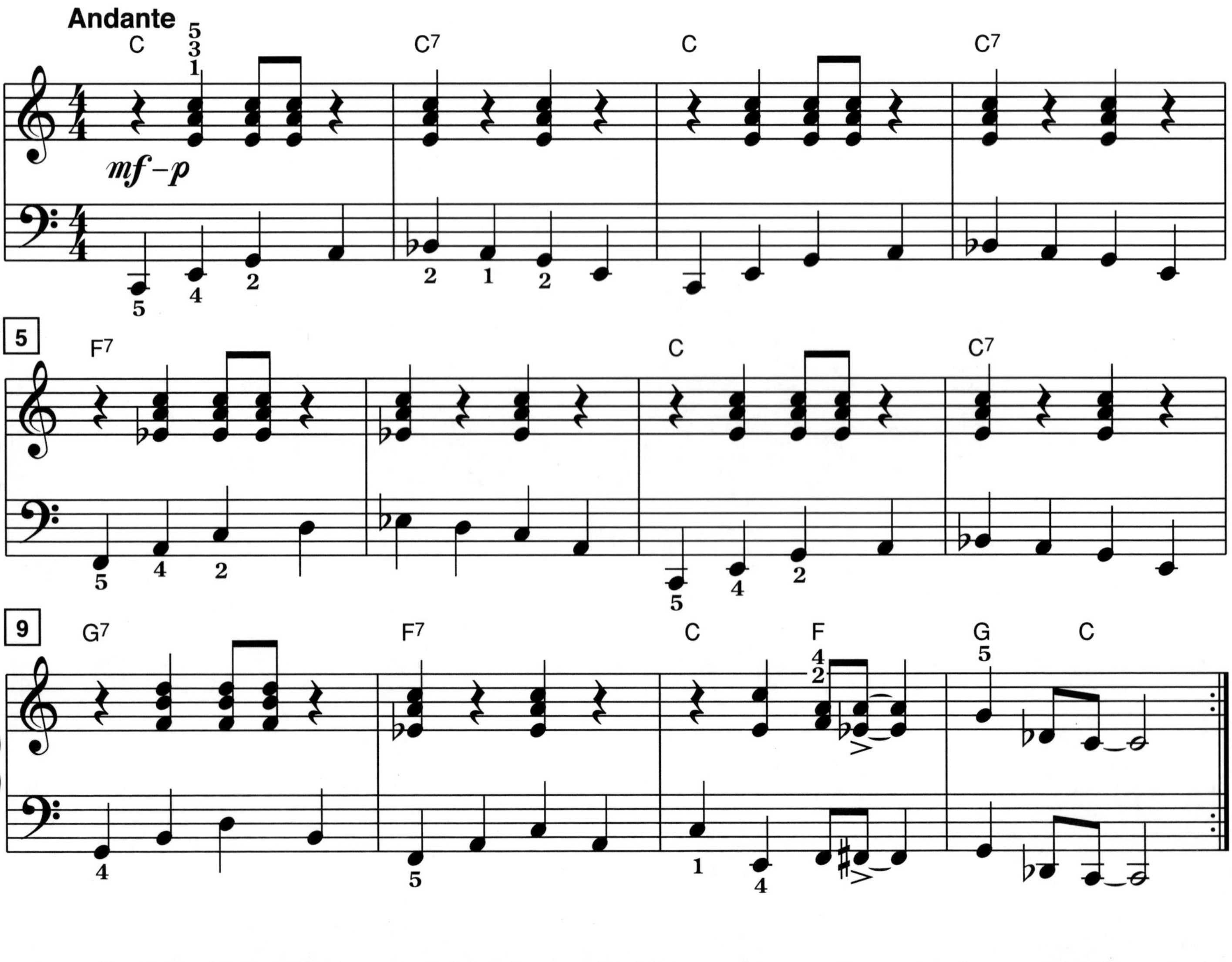

Walking Bass Line in "C"
Performance Piece

Jitterbug Blues

The **walking bass line** offers a strong bass line melody created from **blues scale tones** and **comping chords.** Get your keyboard to *roar* for this one!

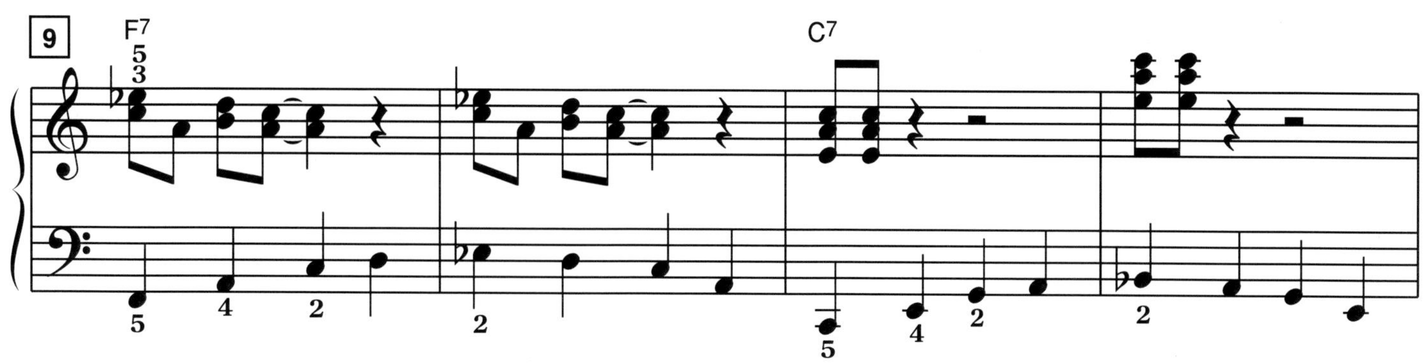

Blues Jam

Eagle City Blues

The melody of this blues progression is stated in the first 12 measures, followed by a written improv over the blues progression chords in measures 13–24. Measures 25–end combine fragments of the melody of **Eagle City Blues** and the improv.

Moderato

Improv

17
F7
C7
21
G7
F7
C
25
C
F7
C7
mp
29
F7
C7
G7
C7
mf
33
G7
F7
C
ritard.

I Feel the Blues in Me!

Express *your* feelings by changing the **dynamics** (louder or softer) wherever you like. This is what blues players do to make their music special.

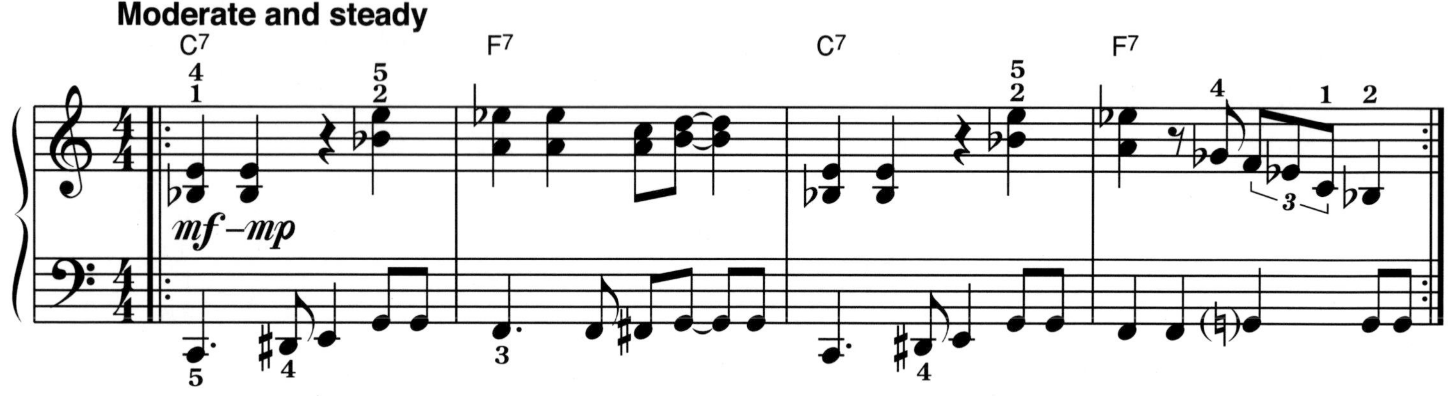

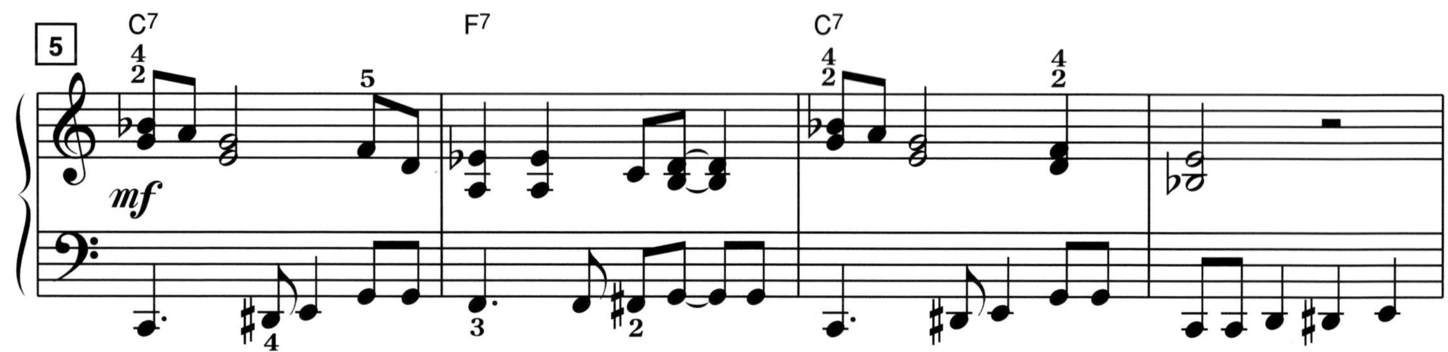

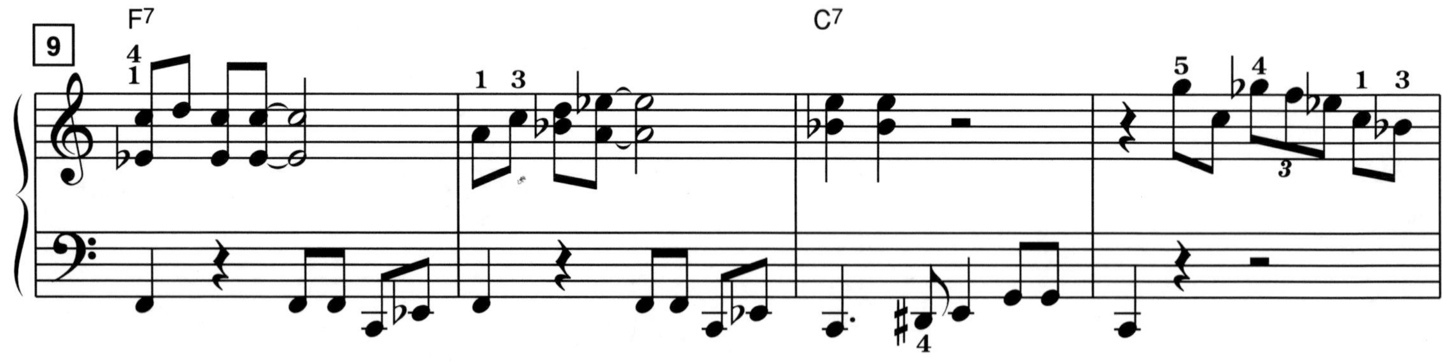

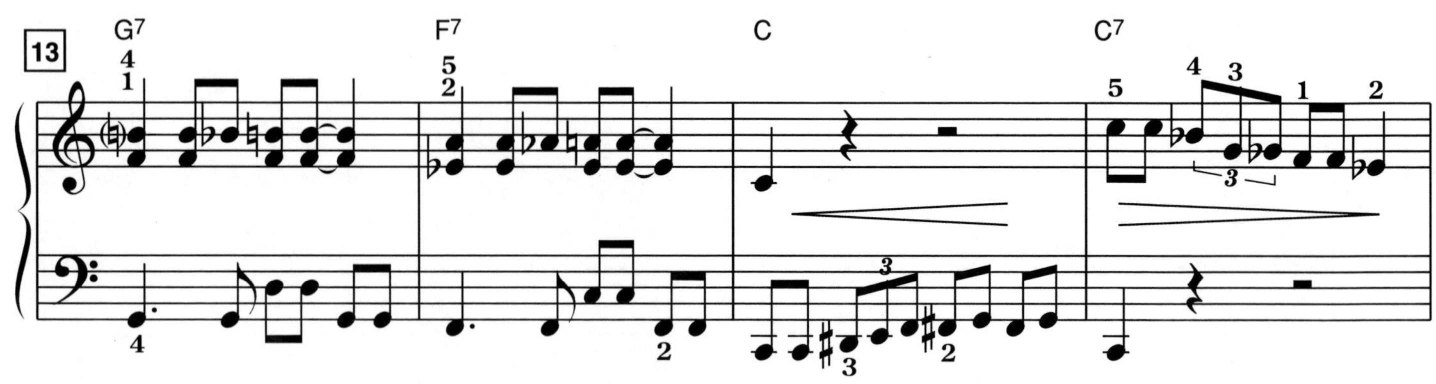

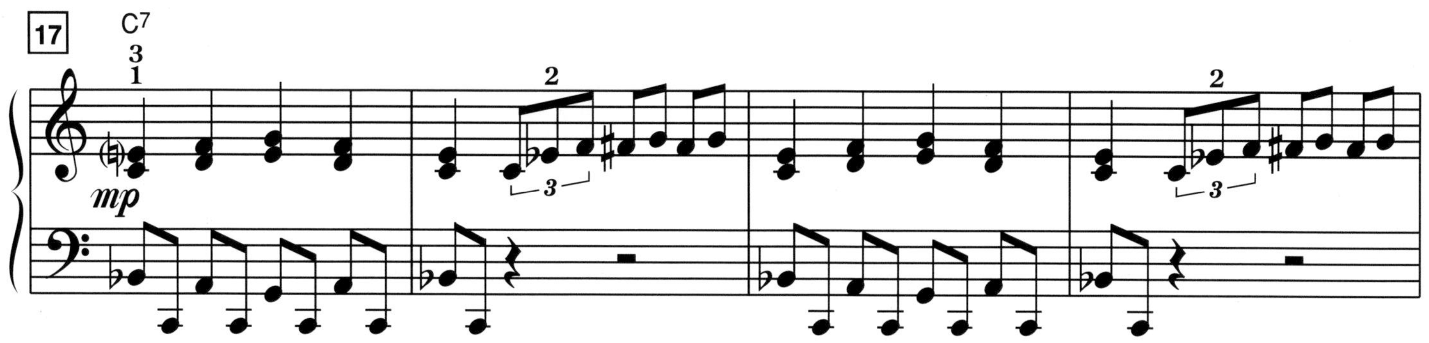
17
C7
mp

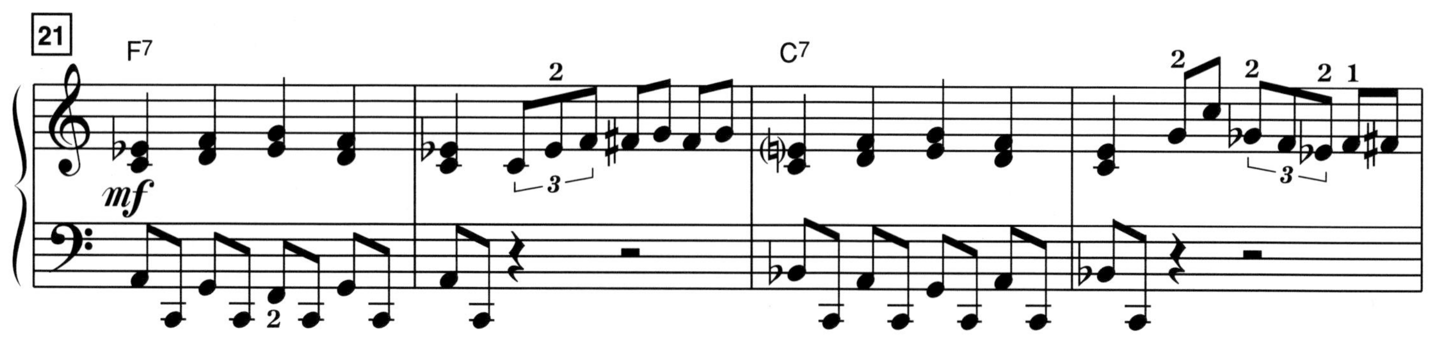
21
F7
mf
C7

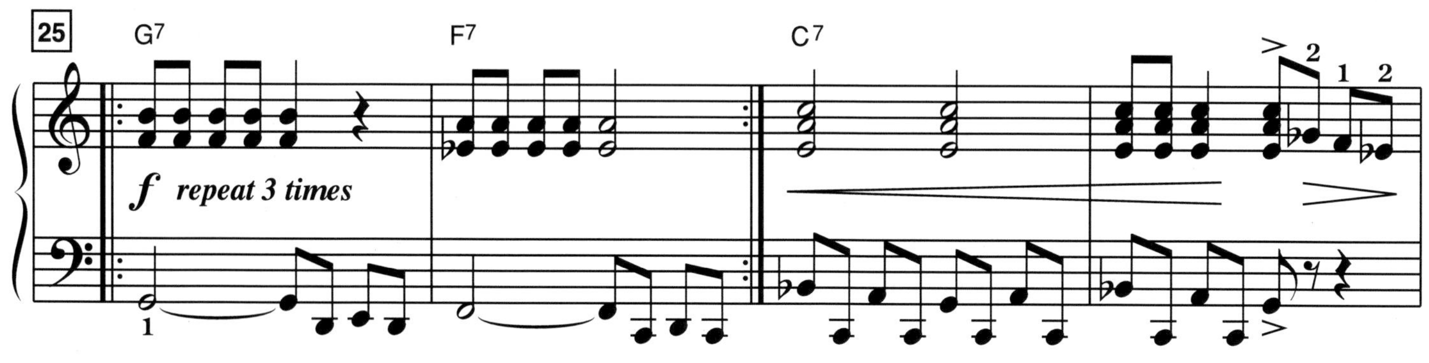
25
G7
F7
C7
f repeat 3 times

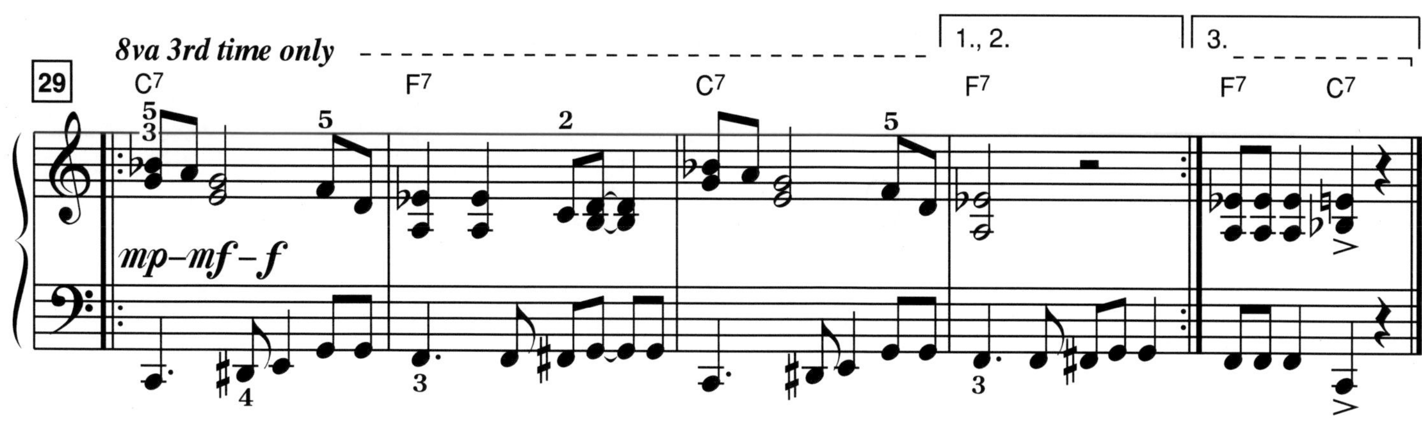
8va 3rd time only
1., 2.
3.
29
C7
F7
C7
F7
F7
C7
mp–mf–f

G Blues Progression & Chord Voicings

The three basic 7th Chords used in the **G blues progression** are:

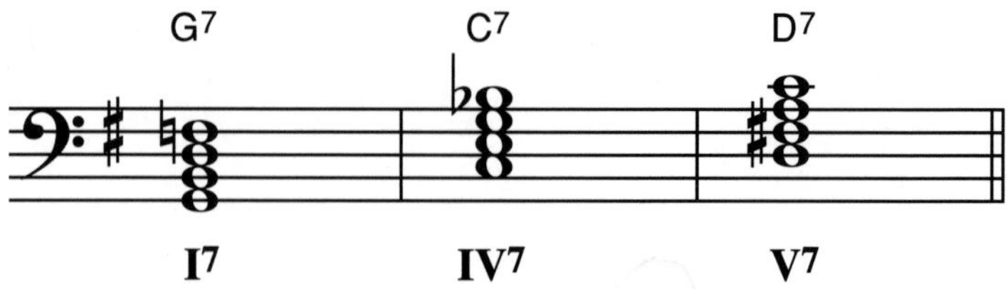

Full Chord Voicing: The re-voicing of the C7 **(IV7)** and D7 **(V7)** chords allow for smoother and easier movement between chords.*

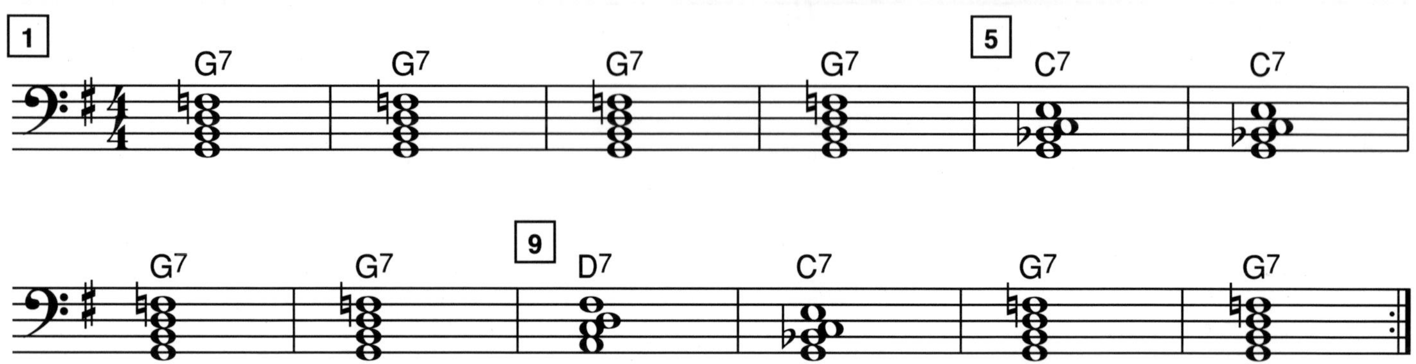

Interval Voicing: In this example, the interval voicing begins with the flatted 7th of the G7 chord in the bass with the 3rd above it. The voicings following it are selected to create the least amount of movement between tones.*

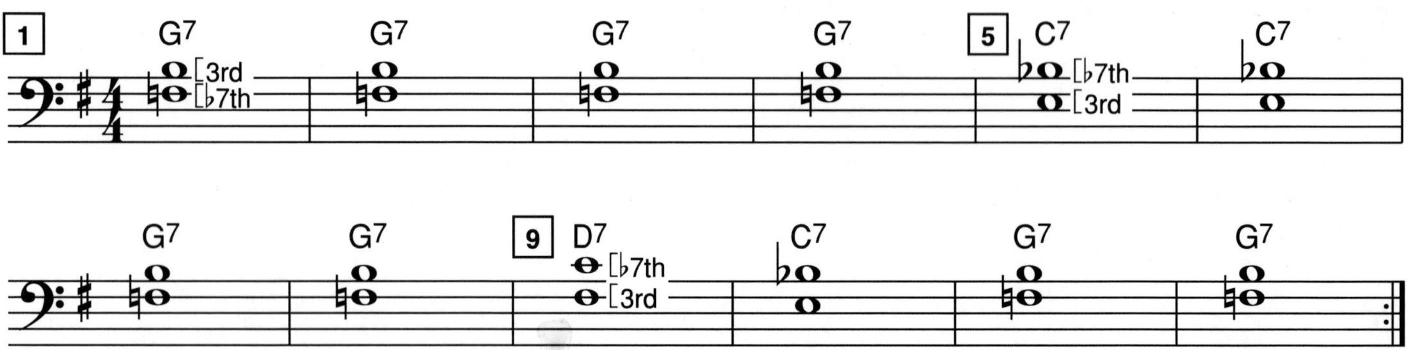

*Practice the full chord and interval voicings slowly until memorized.

G Blues Progression Performance Piece

Lazy Day Blues

Careful use of the pedal will help to create the special bluesy mood that this blues sets. Play it real slow, dragging out the last measure as much as you can. Notice that a slight variation in the blues progression occurs in measures 11–14.

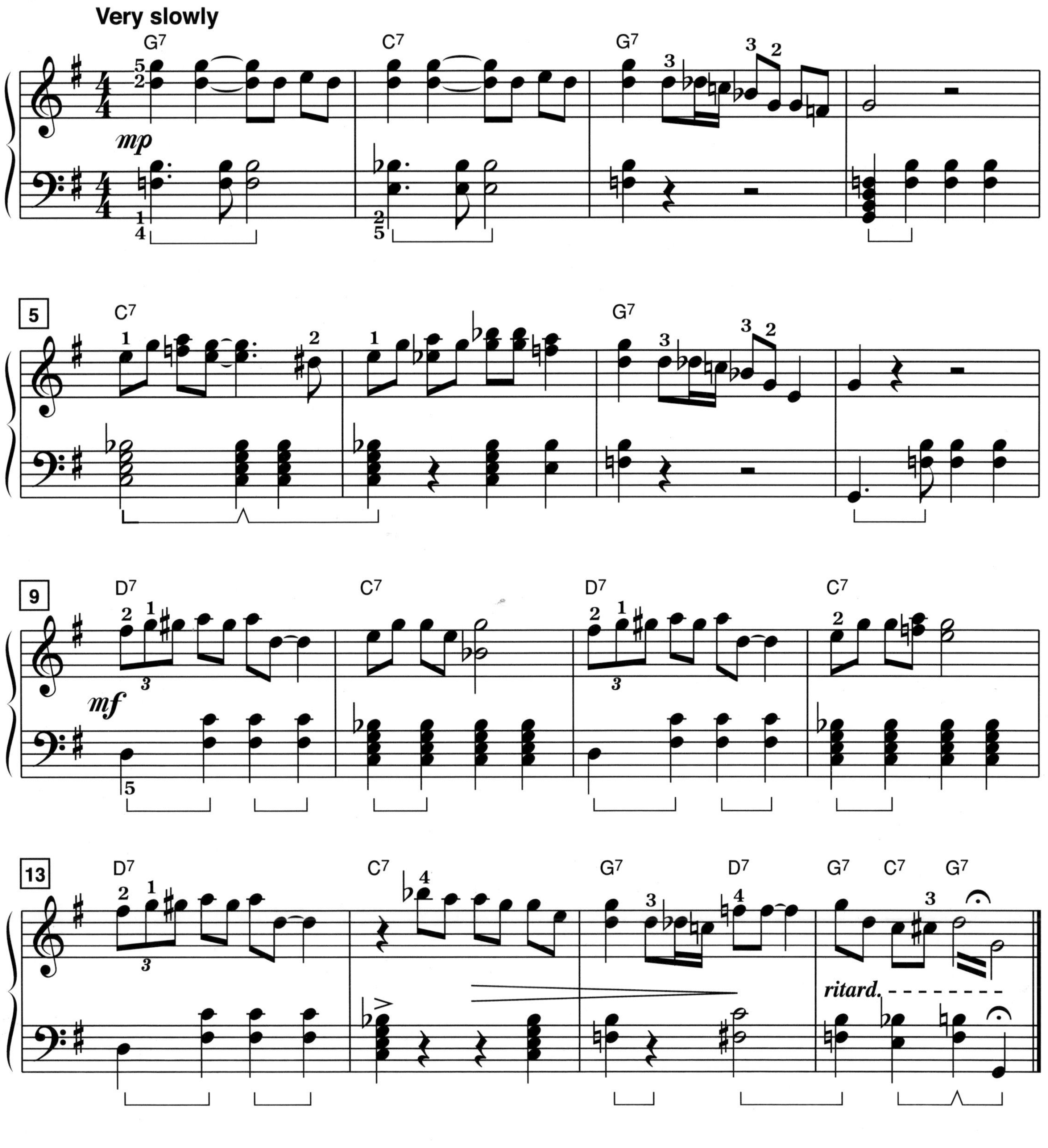

Very slowly

G7 C7 G7

5 C7 G7

9 D7 C7 D7 C7

13 D7 C7 G7 D7 G7 C7 G7

ritard.

Walking Bass Line in "G"

This "G" **walking bass line** gains rhythmic punch by adding eighth notes.

G
G7
G
G7
5
C
C7
G
G7
9
D
C
G

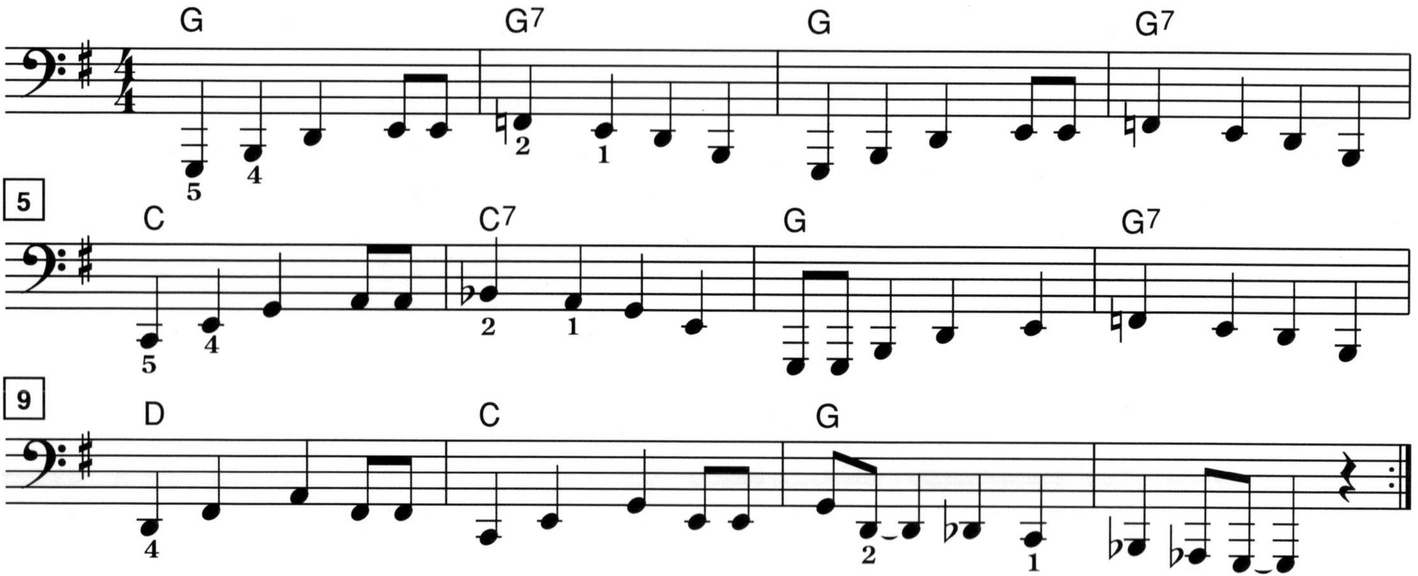

Getting Together Blues

A **comping pattern** is used here as a repeated rhythmic figure over the "G" walking bass line.

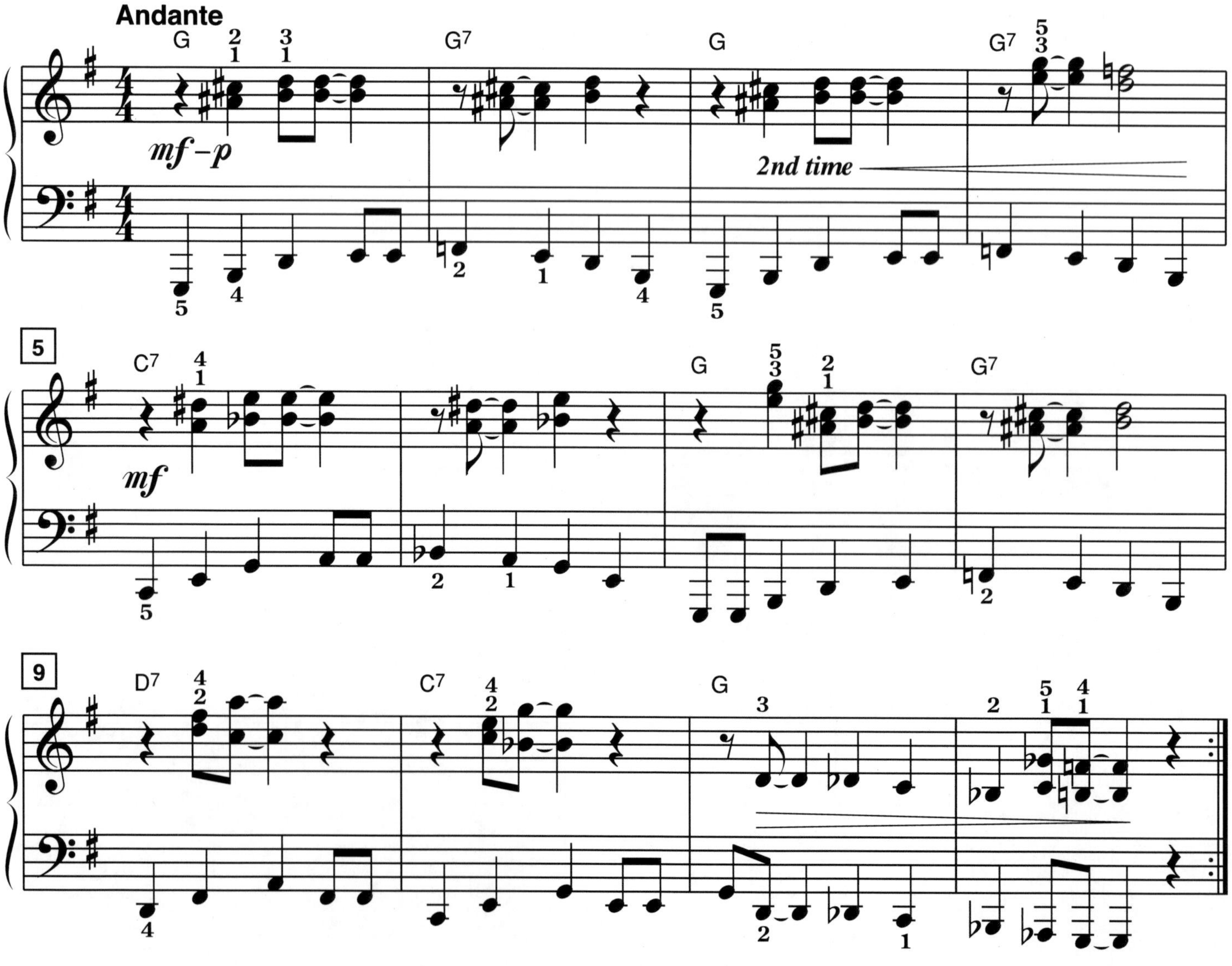

Andante
G
G7
G
G7
mf–p
2nd time
5
C7
G
G7
mf
9
D7
C7
G

Walking Bass Line in "G" Performance Piece

Whistle-stop Blues

Track 25

The "G" **walking bass line** (measures 1–12) and the **double-note boogie bass** (measures 13–18) set up a background for a **comping pattern** in the right hand. All aboard for a ride into blues country!

The G Blues Scale

The **G Blues Scale** is created by using exactly the same intervals between tones as was used in constructing the C Blues Scale. Practice each hand separately in both ascending and descending order.

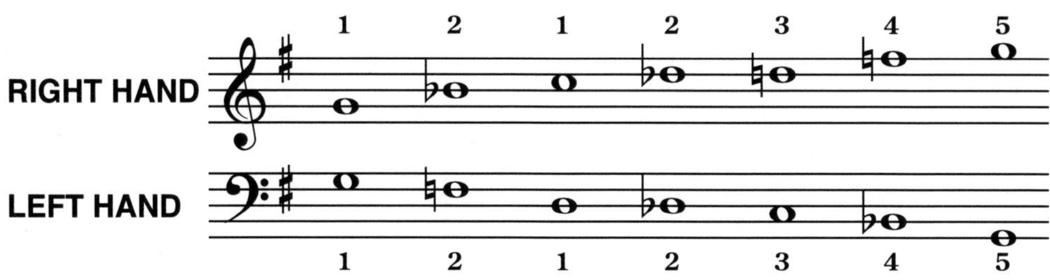

The Things Can Change Blues

The **G blues scale** creates a blues feeling here even though the blues chord progression is not used. Sometimes **Things Can Change** in music without upsetting the basic mood of a composition.

Track 26

Heavy

Gm

f–p

8va

D7

Gm7 C7 D7 Gm7 C7 D7

f *last time, fade out*

Gm C7 Gm D7

D. C. al Fade out

G Blues Scale Performance Piece

The **grace note** (𝅘𝅥𝅮) is an important musical ornament that is used in the Blues to simulate the special sound of the guitar and banjo. It is played here with the neighboring finger.

Firefly Blues

Strike the grace note quickly, before the beat, with the indicated finger.

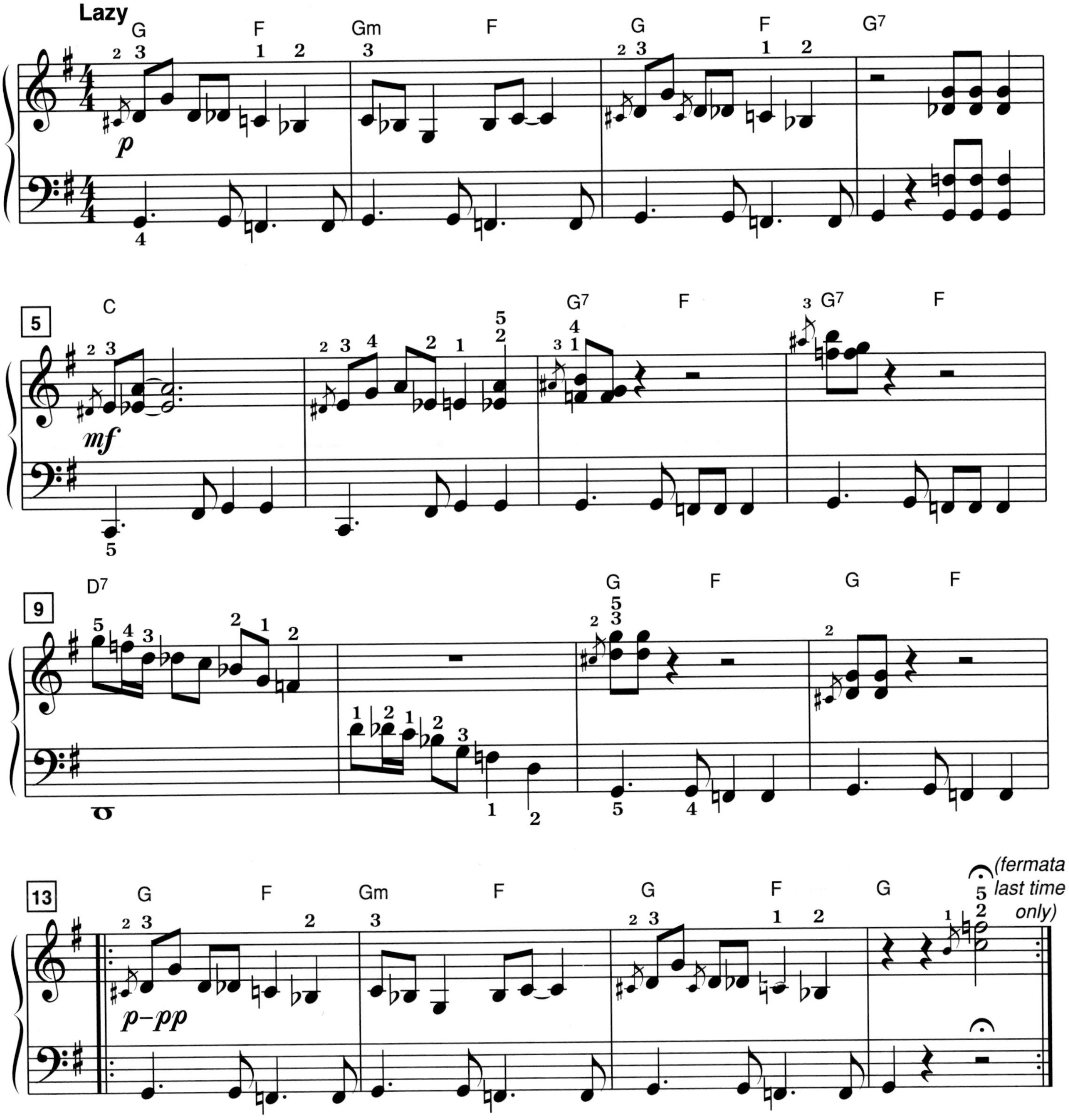

Lazy

G F Gm F G F G7

5 C G7 F G7 F

9 D7 G F G F

13 G F Gm F G F G

(fermata last time only)

Blue Notes—G Scale

The Blue Notes (*) in the G Scale are B♭ (flatted 3rd), D♭ (flatted 5th) and F♮ (flatted 7th).

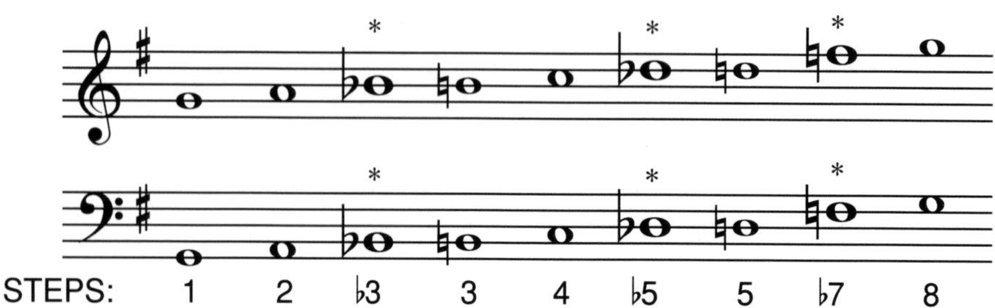

Reaching Out for the Blues

Flatted 3rd, 5th and **7th blue notes** in the right hand are joined by left-hand chords using flatted 7ths to reinforce a bluesy sound.

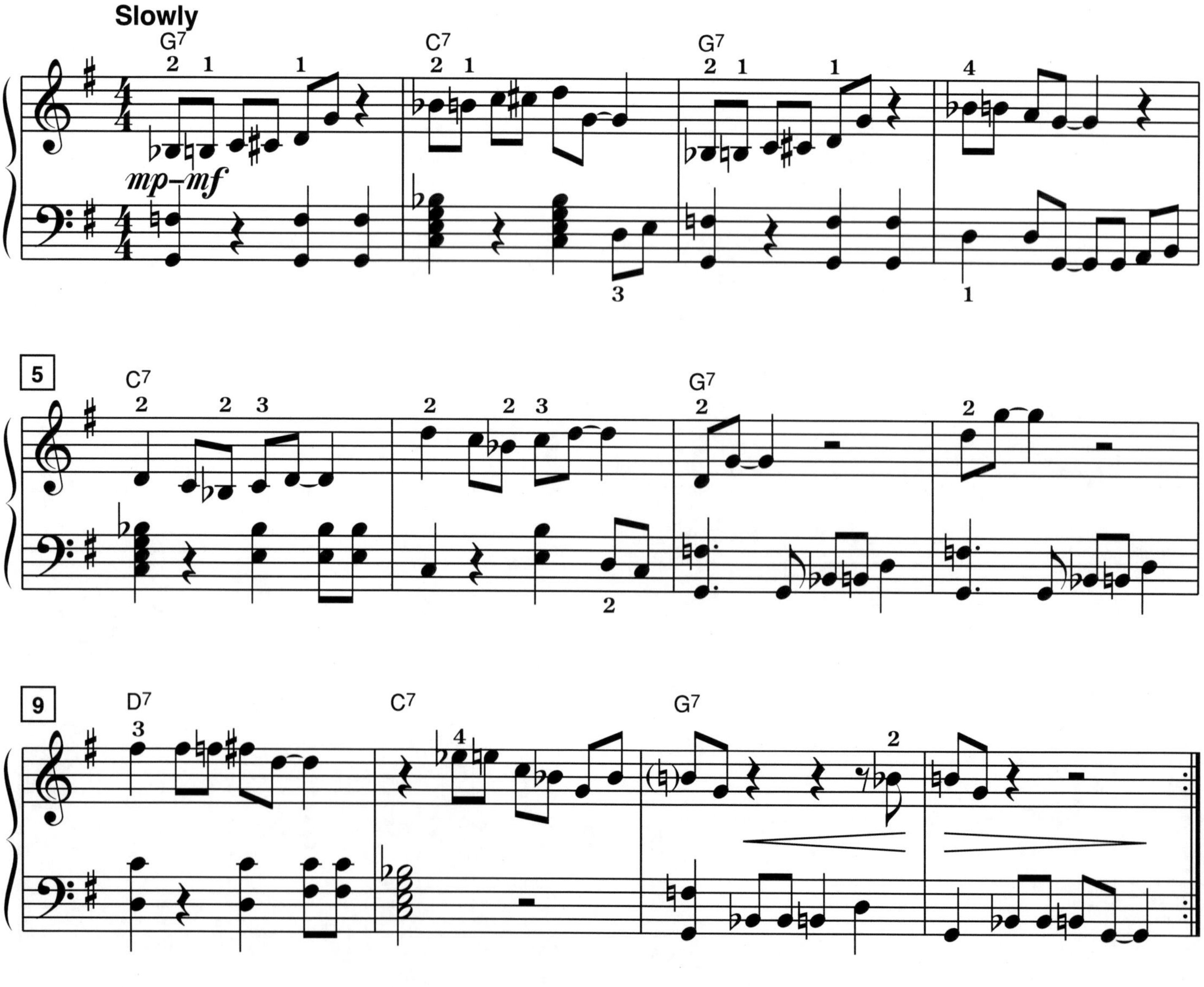

Slowly

G7 C7 G7

mp–mf

5 C7 G7

9 D7 C7 G7

Blue Notes Performance Piece—G Scale

Seventh Avenue Blues

This lazy feeling composition creates a special blues sound and feeling by using blue notes in the G scale.

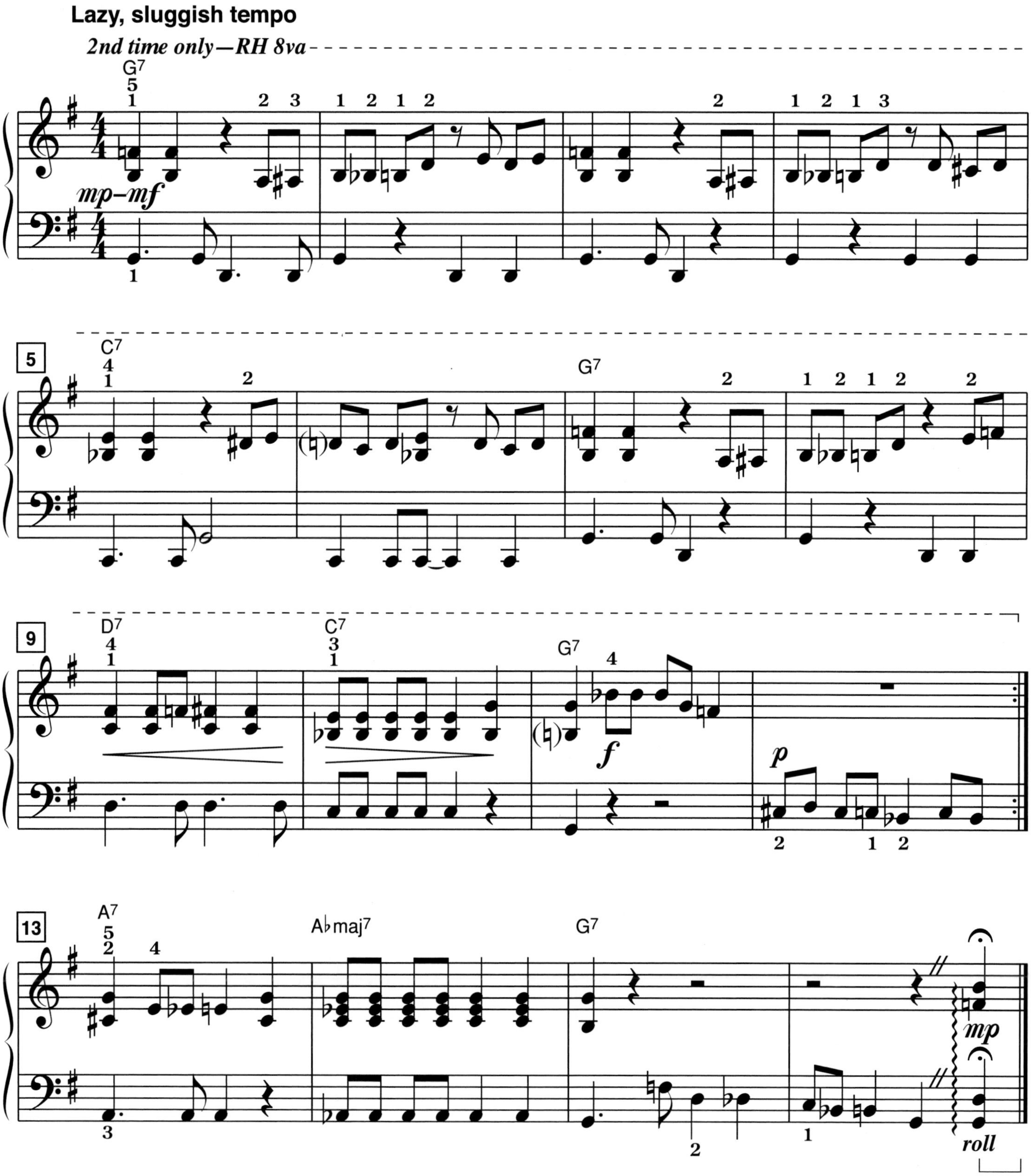

Lazy, sluggish tempo

2nd time only—RH 8va

G7 — C7 — G7 — D7 — C7 — G7 — A7 — A♭maj7 — G7

mp–mf *f* *p* *mp* *roll*

G Blue Notes & Blues Scale Performance Piece

Slippin' and Slidin'

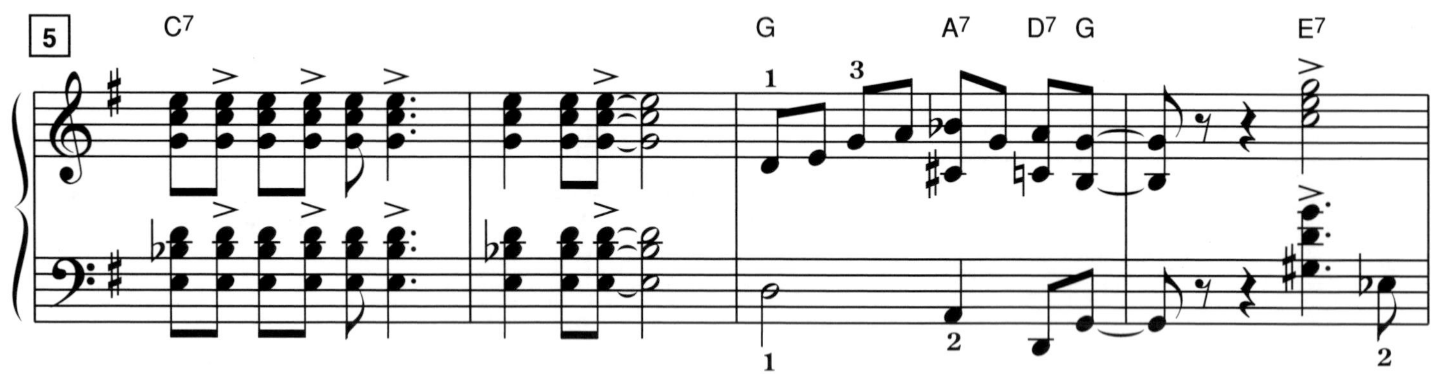

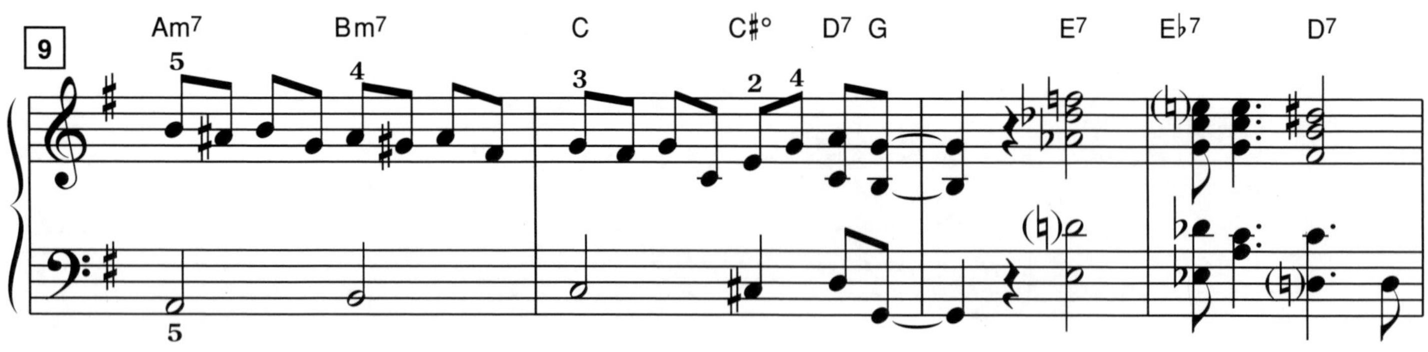

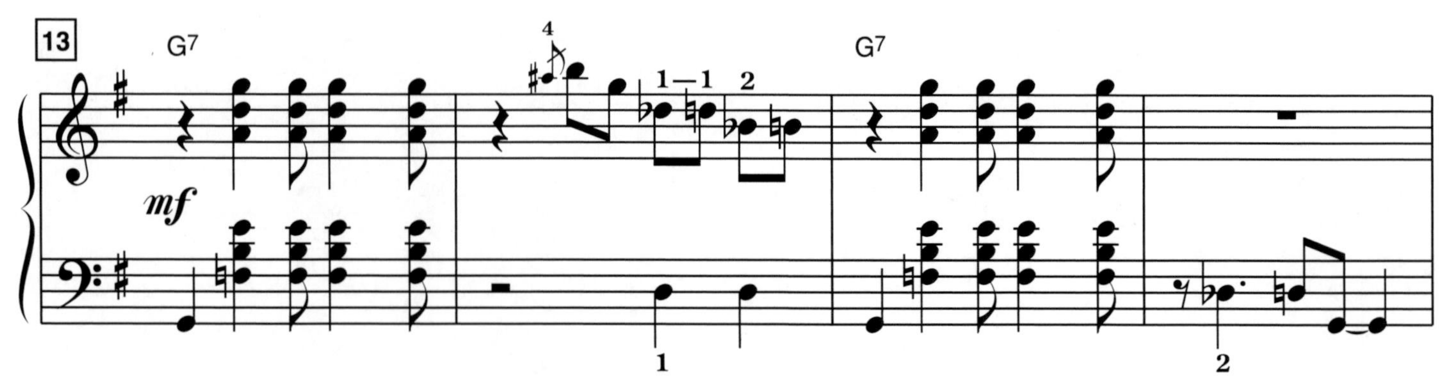

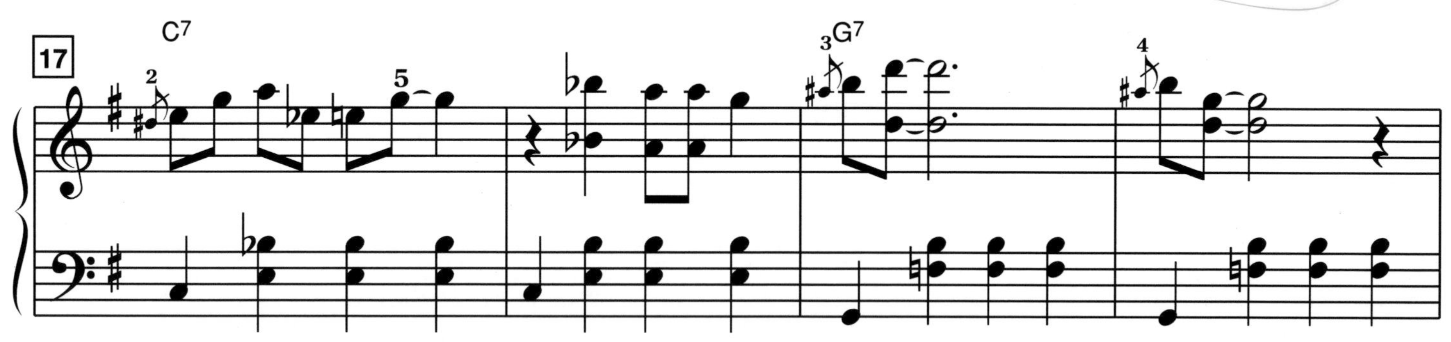
17
C7
G7

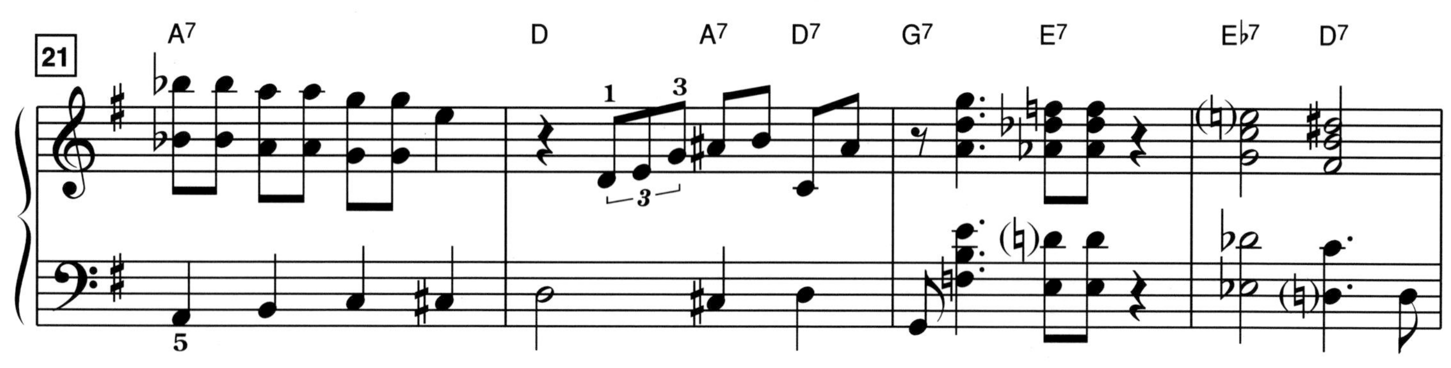
21
A7
D
A7
D7
G7
E7
E♭7
D7

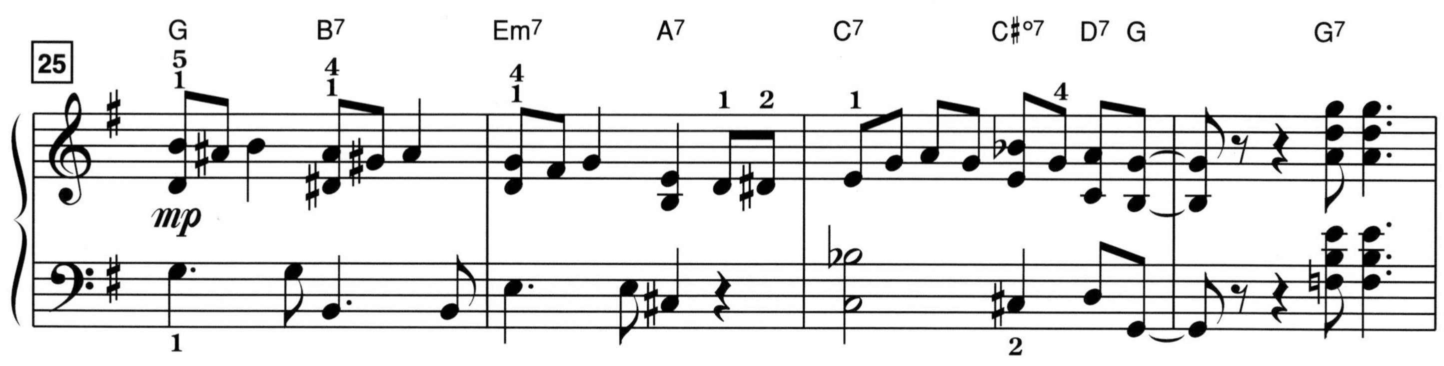
25
G
B7
Em7
A7
C7
C♯°7
D7
G
G7
mp

29
C7
C♯°7
D7
G
G7
f-p-f
repeat 3 times—ritard.
last time
f

F Blues Progression & Chord Voicings

The three basic Seventh Chords used in the **F Blues Progression** are:

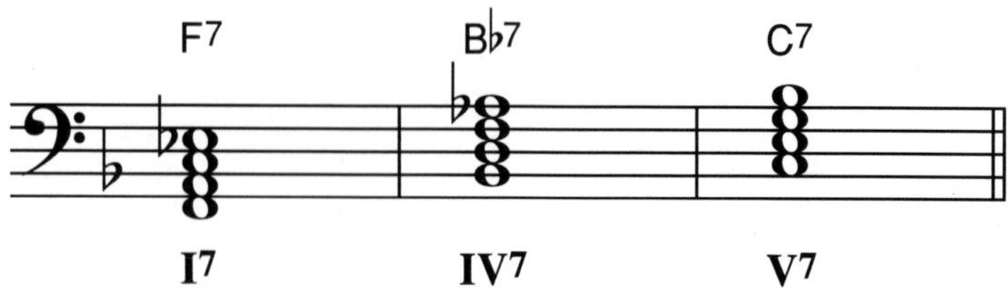

Full Chord Voicing: The re-voicing of the B♭7 **(IV7)** and C7 **(V7)** chords allow for smoother and easier movement between chords.*

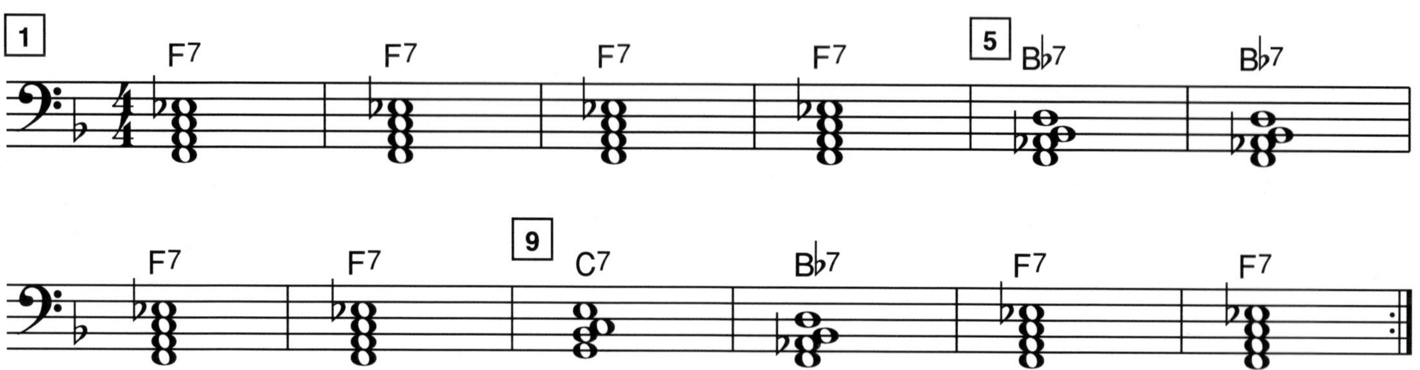

Interval Voicing: In this example, the interval voicing begins with the 3rd of the F7 chord in the bass with the flatted 7th above it. The voicings following it are selected to create the least amount of movement between tones.*

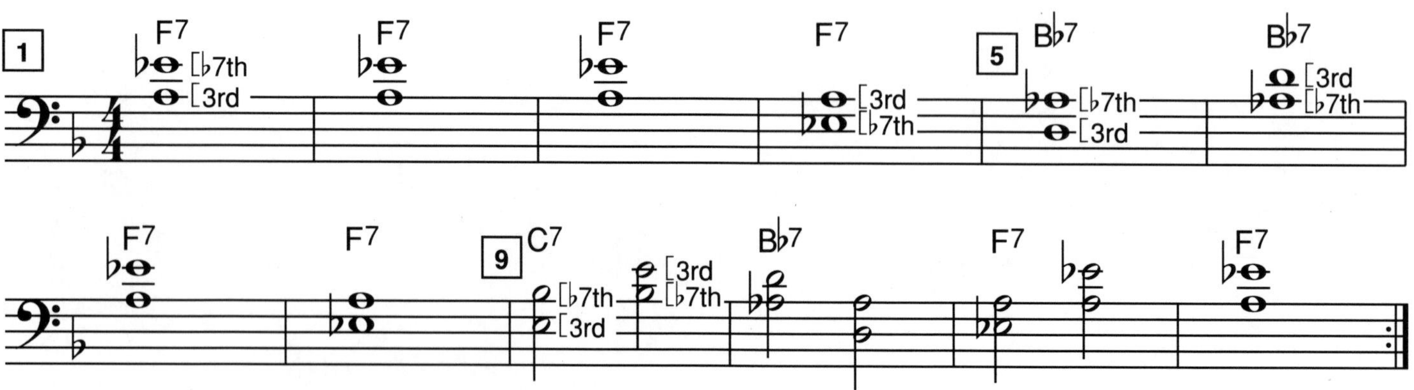

*Practice the full chord and interval voicings slowly until memorized.

F Blues Progression Performance Piece

The Hurry Up and Wait Blues

A variety of full chord and interval voicings challenge the left hand to add a strong accompaniment to the melody in the right hand.

Andante

repeat and fade out

B♭7 *fermata last time only*

Walking Bass Line in "F"

The **F walking bass line** now uses a slightly modified set of chords as well as descending and ascending motion in order to gain greater variety. In this example, *half-steps, skips, rests* and *changes in direction* create a bass line like those often played by blues bass players in a band.

All Together

Learn the Walking Bass Line in "F" and then play this slow-moving blues in an easygoing manner.

Slow moving

Walking Bass Line in "F" Performance Piece

Bass Players' Blues

The "F" Walking Bass Line appears in a slightly altered rhythmic version. Measures 9–20 features a solo for the bass player as is usually found in a Blues band. Make the left hand sound like a bass solo by playing the comping right hand very soft and short.

Gentle, easy manner

Fine

(LH solo)

D. C. al Fine

The F Blues Scale

The **F Blues Scale** is created by using exactly the same intervals between tones as was used in constructing the C and G Blues Scales. Practice each hand separately in both ascending and descending order.

RIGHT HAND
LEFT HAND

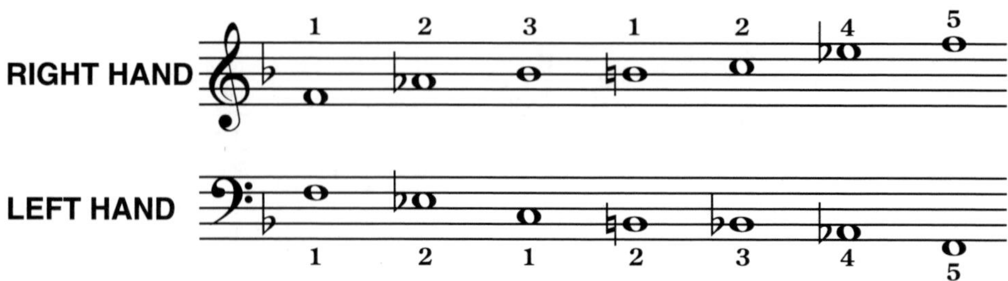

Dot Matrix

The **F Blues Scale** is combined with a strong rhythmic bass line, adding a contemporary blues feeling to the traditional sounds of a blues melody.

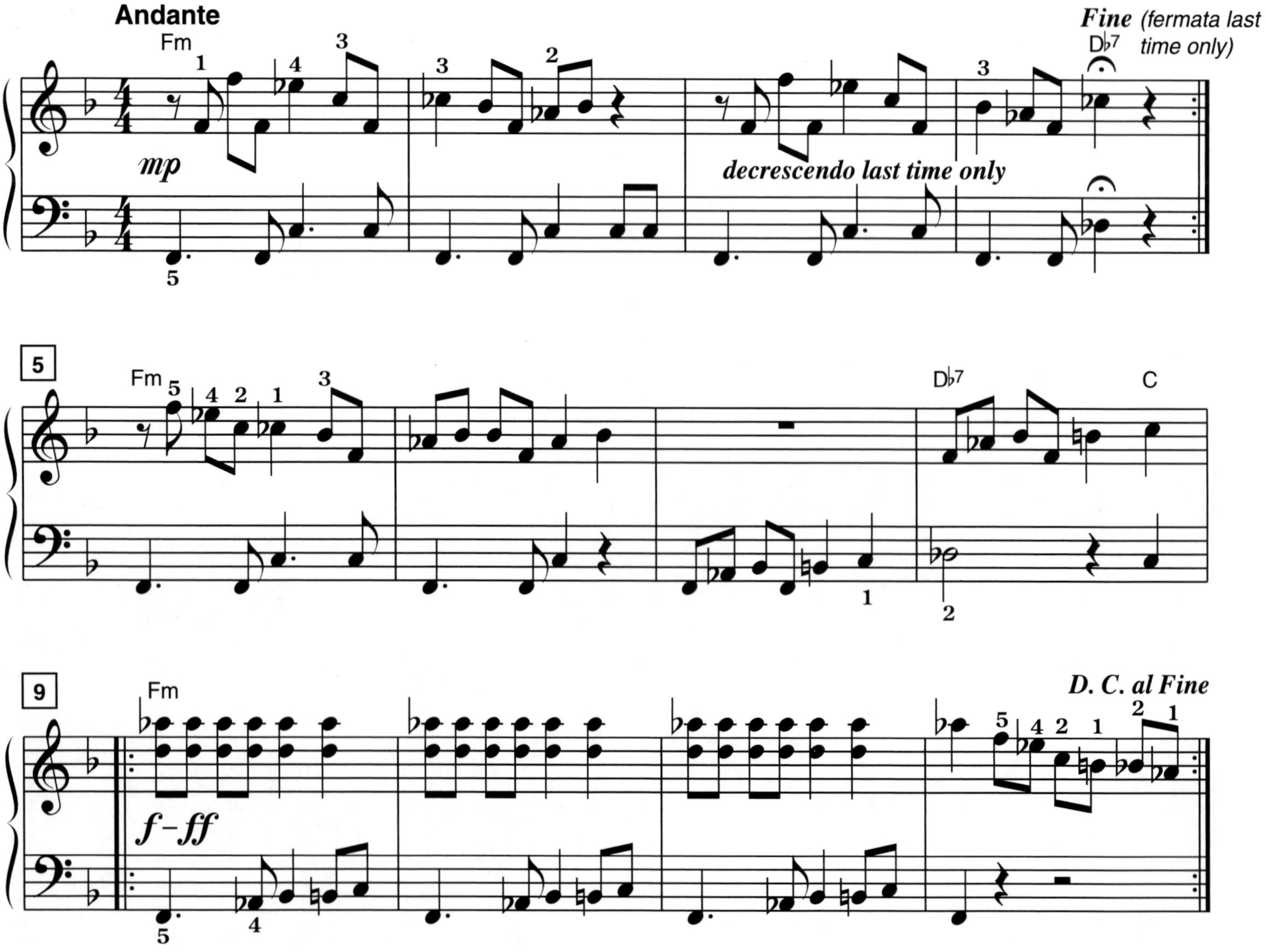

Andante
Fm
Fine (fermata last time only)
D♭7
mp
decrescendo last time only
5
Fm
D♭7
C
9
Fm
D. C. al Fine
f–ff

F Blues Scale Performance Piece

MINI MUSIC LESSON

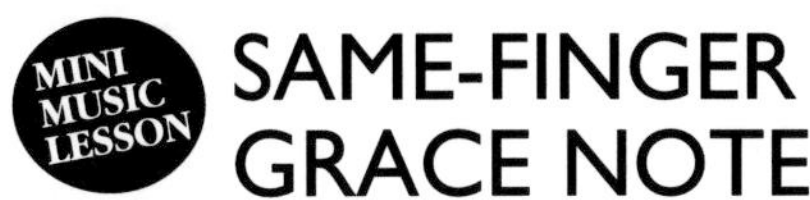

SAME-FINGER GRACE NOTE

The blues **grace note** is sometimes played using the *same* finger that then slides to its neighboring tone. The slight delay of the grace note caused by the slower finger movement helps to create a more "twangy" sound.

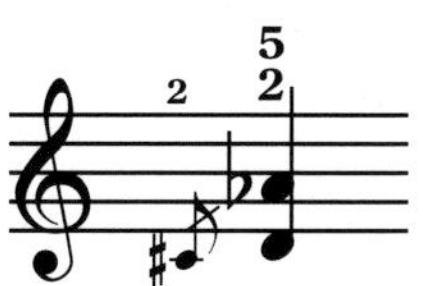

Back Country Blues

Track 33

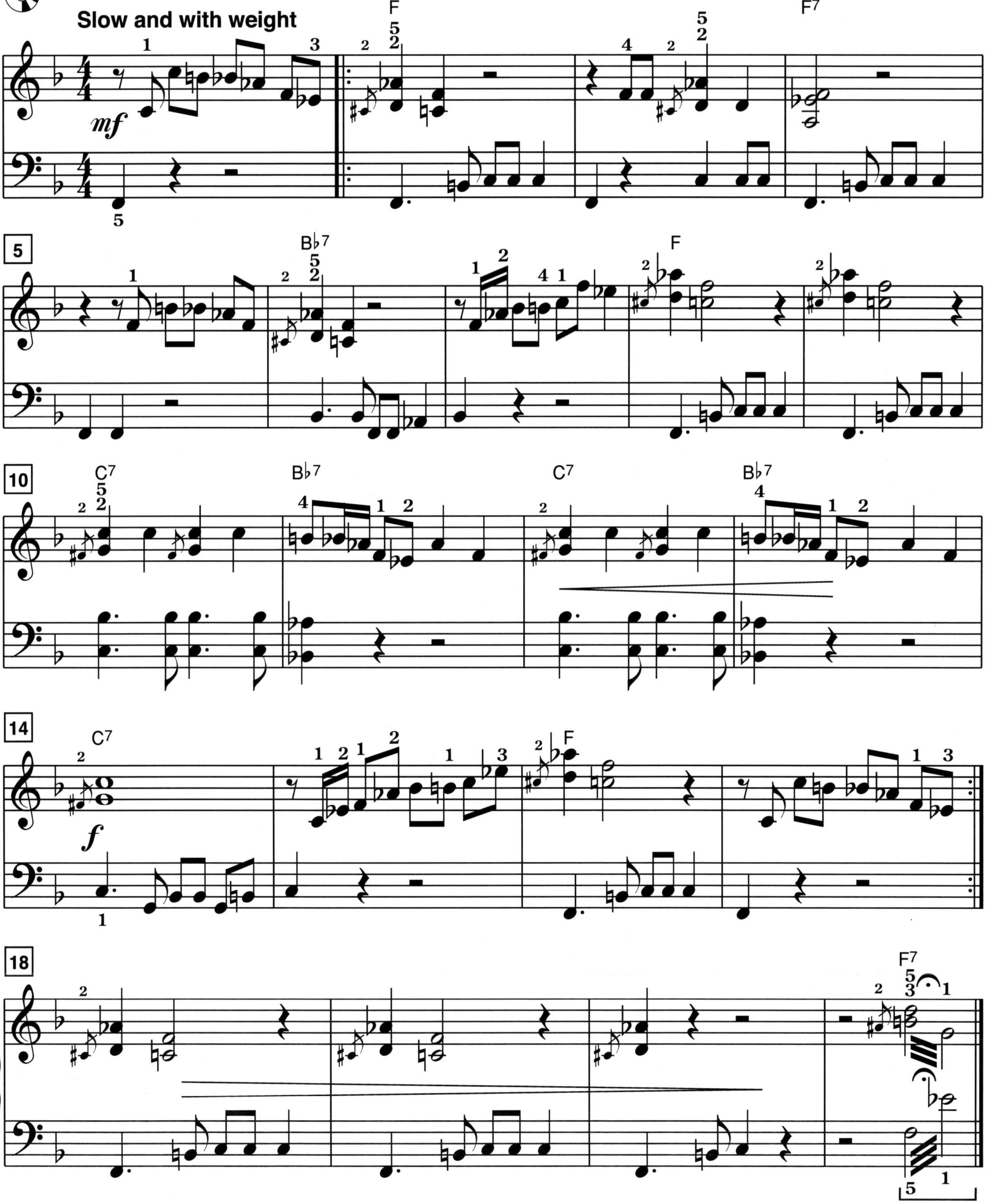

Slow and with weight
mf
F
F7
B♭7
F
C7
B♭7
C7
B♭7
C7
f
F
F7

Blue Notes—F Scale

The Blue Notes (*) in the F Scale are A♭ (flatted 3rd), C♭ (flatted 5th) and E♭ (flatted 7th).

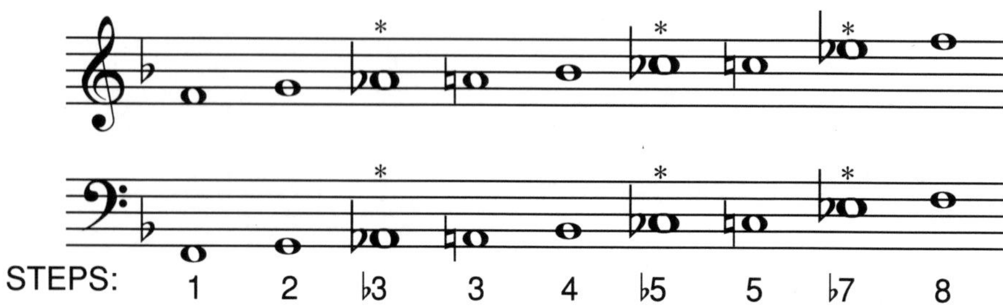

String of Pearls

Blue notes combine here with right-hand chords that are *voiced* in intervals of 3rds and 4ths* to create a contemporary blues sound. There are many interesting chords here—spend some extra time learning them.

Moderately slow

F B♭ D♭ F Dm D♭7 Cm7

mf–p

5 F B♭7 B° F Dm B°7 Cm7 F7

9 Bm7(♭5) B♭m7 F A♭7 G7 F B° C7 F7

f *p* *mp* *ritard. last time*

Blue Notes Performance Piece—F Scale

Don't Rush Me Blues

Like the title says, this lazy blues needs plenty of time and space. Blue notes, flatted-3rd grace notes and groovy chords offer you a chance to sound like an authentic blues player.

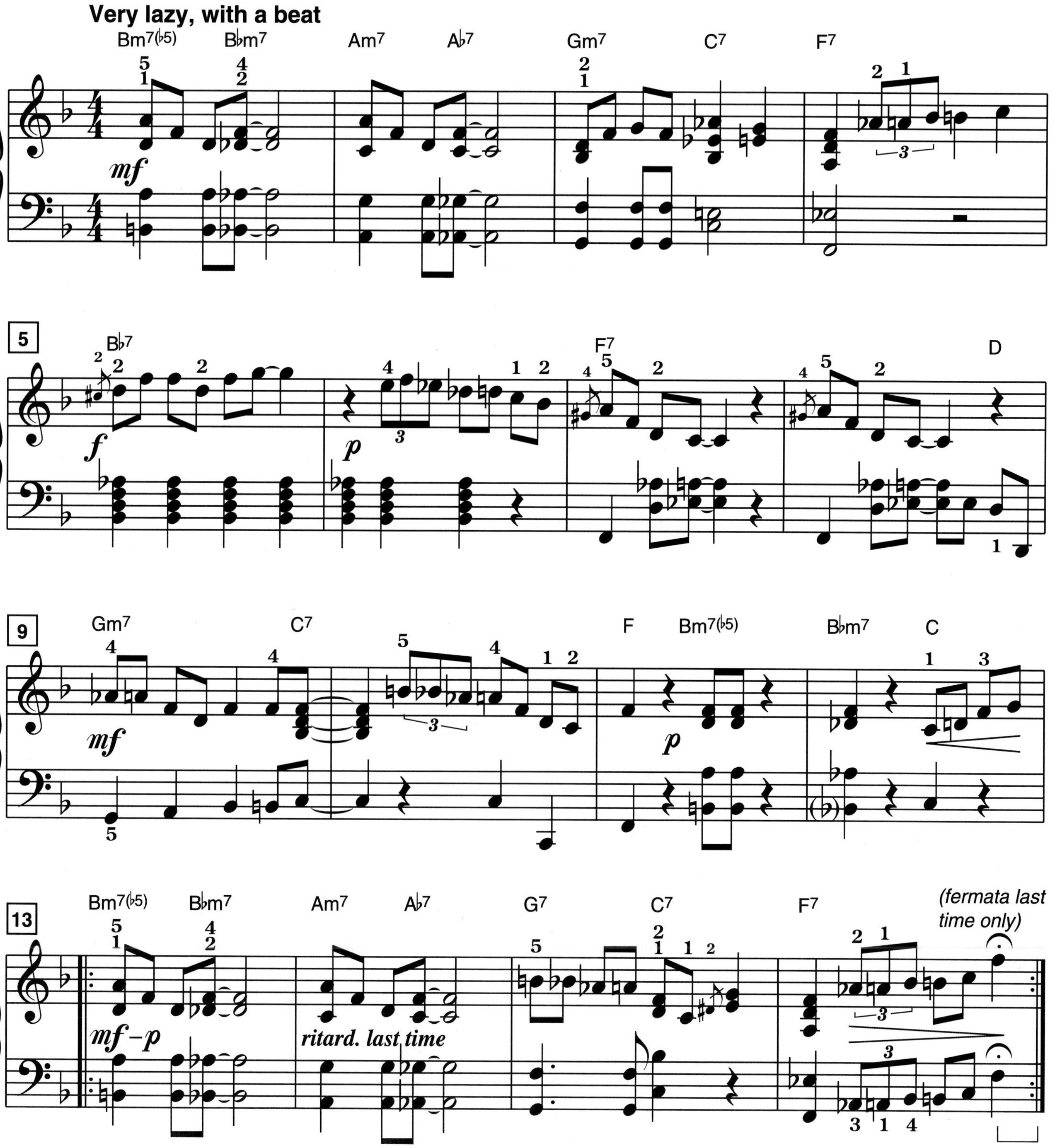

Very lazy, with a beat

Bm7(♭5) B♭m7 Am7 A♭7 Gm7 C7 F7

5 B♭7 F7 D

9 Gm7 C7 F Bm7(♭5) B♭m7 C

13 Bm7(♭5) B♭m7 Am7 A♭7 G7 C7 F7

mf–p *ritard. last time*

(fermata last time only)

Blues Jam

Blues for Sassy

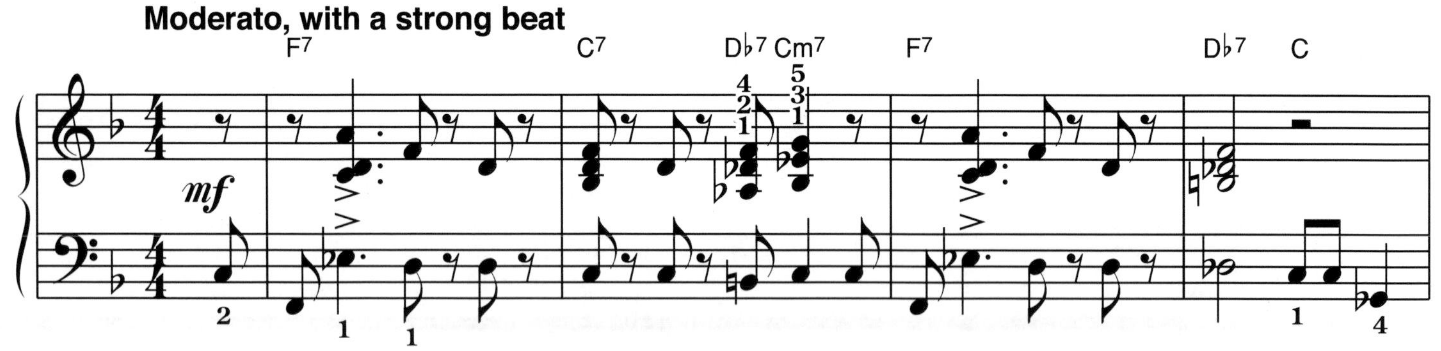

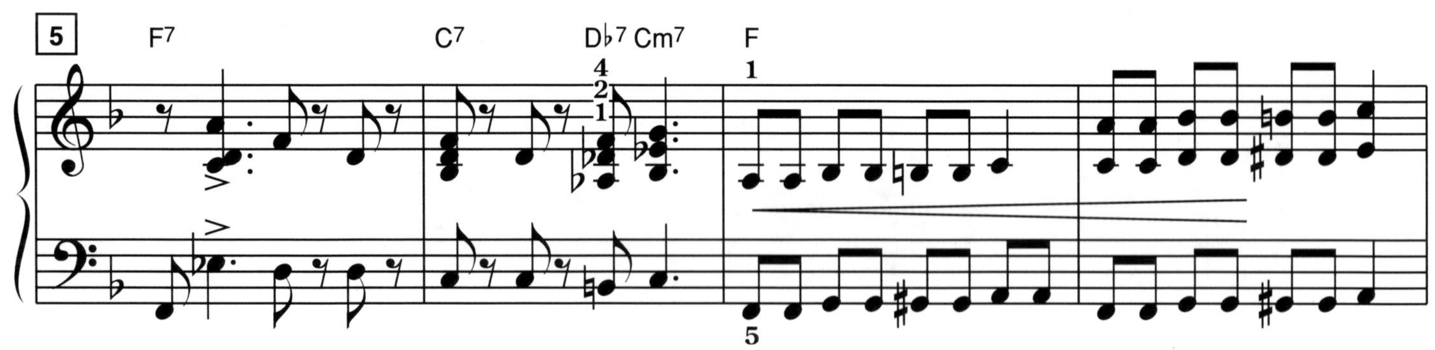

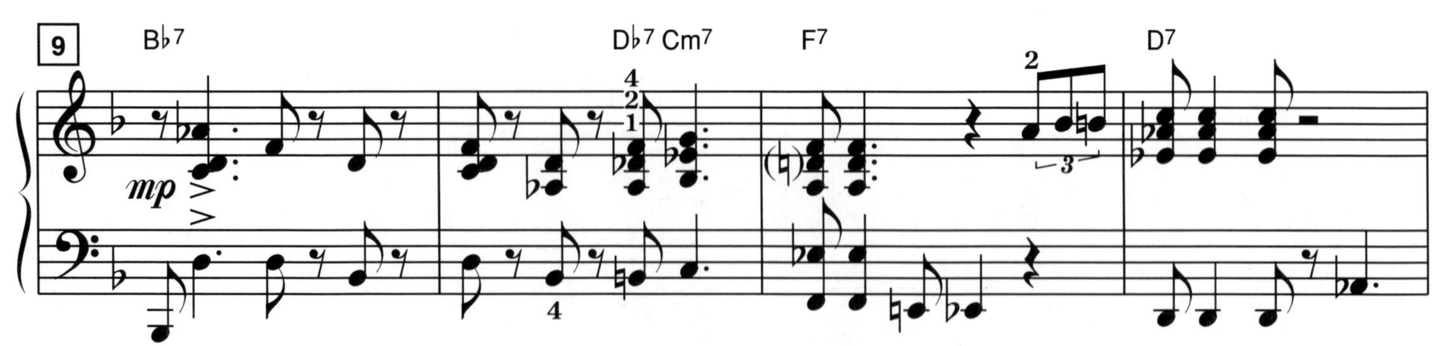

17
F7
B♭7
F7
mf
21
B♭7
F7
Dm7(♭5)
25
G7
C
D♭7 Cm7
F
A♭
G
G♭
29
F7
C7
D♭7 Cm7
F7
D♭7
C
mp
33
F7
C7
D♭7 Cm7
F
G
G♭
F7

Call and Response & the F Boogie Bass

Call and response is a musical technique that has its roots in the spirituals, then the blues and on to jazz and rock. A repeated statement (the call) is answered each time by another repeated or slightly different idea (response). When call and response meet a boogie bass … well, **That's the Blues!**

That's the Blues!

With a steady beat

F — *mf* (call) — (response)

5 — B♭7 — F

9 — Gm7 — C — F — *Fine*

13 — F — *f–p* — B♭ — F — B♭

D. C. al Fine

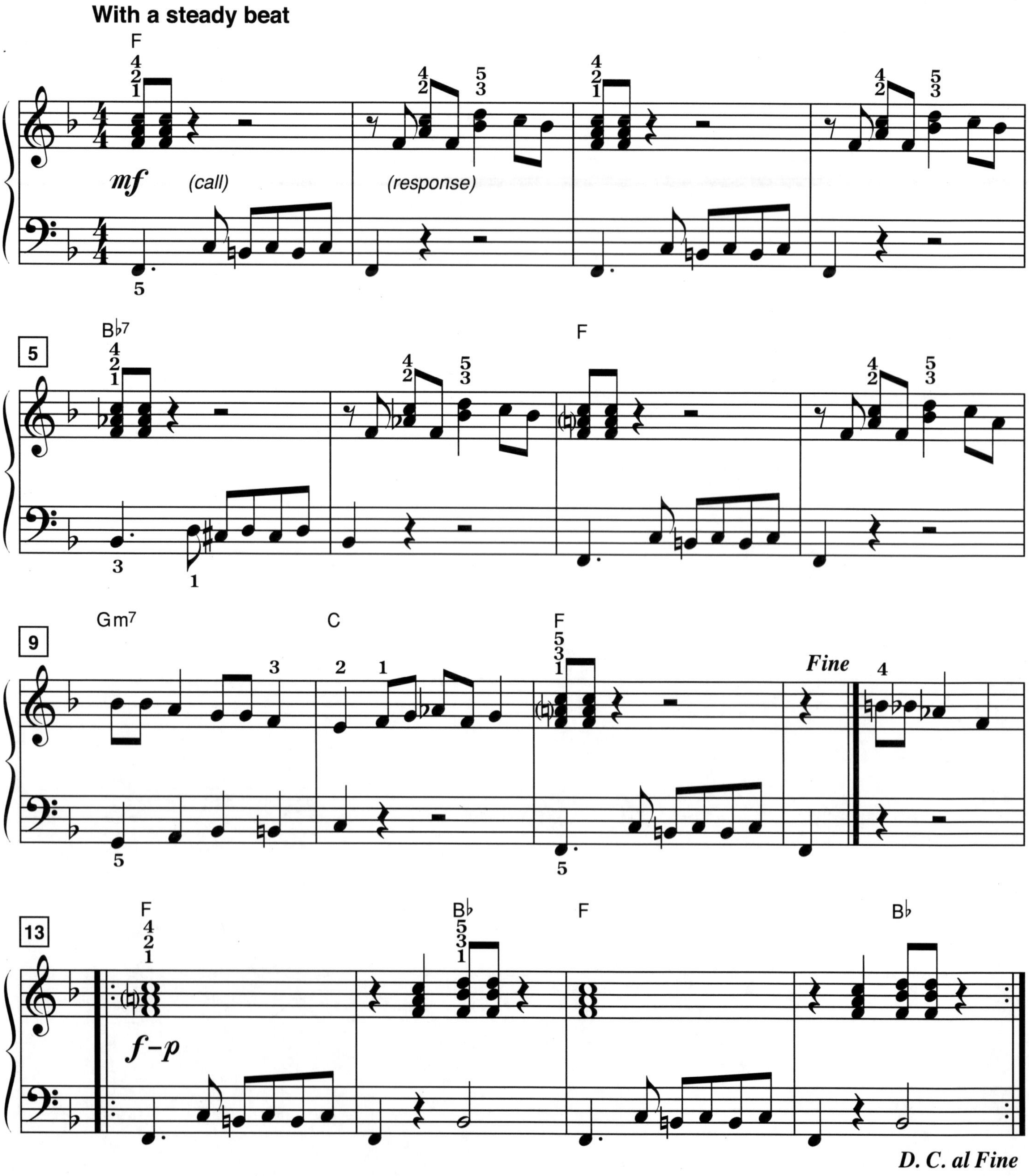

Call and Response with an F Rock Bass

Sound Off!

Turn up the volume and let this typical rock bass carry you through this roaring **Call and Response Blues Progression.** Count off, then Sound Off!

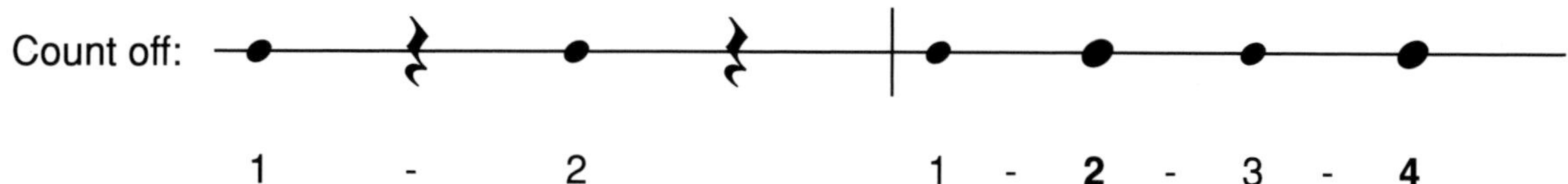

Steady, moderately slow

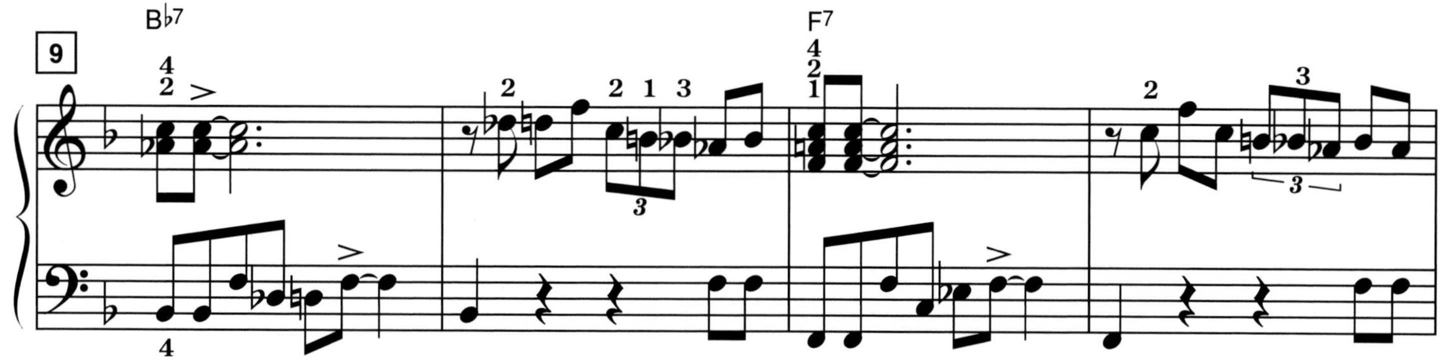

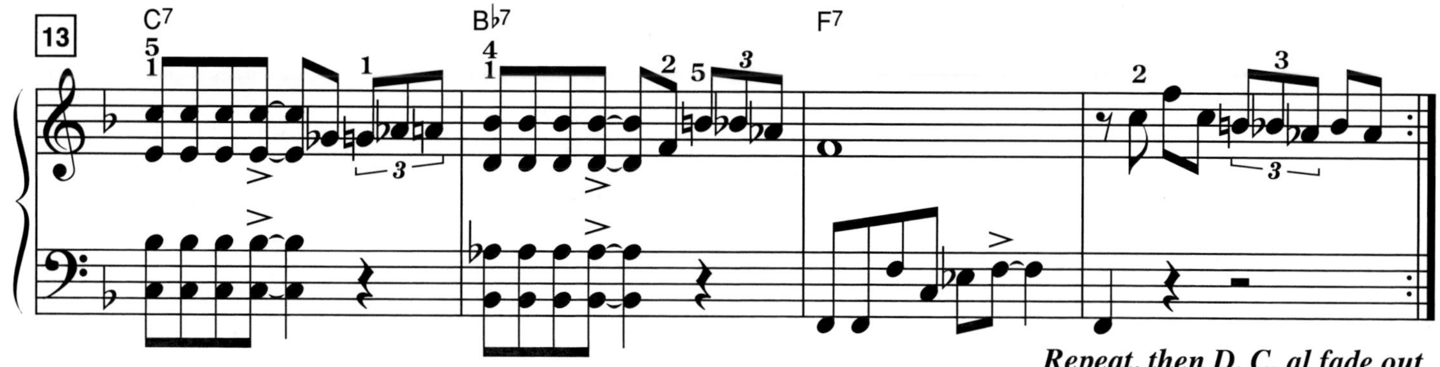

Repeat, then D. C. al fade out

Blue Notes & Blues Scale Performance Piece

The Saints Go Marching In Blues

21
N.C.
B°7
B♭7
D7
25
Slower and proudly!
G
C
G
C
G
29
B7
Em
A7
D7
33
G7
C7
C♯°7
37
G
Em
A7
D7
repeat 3 times—play RH
an ocatave lower 2nd time
C7
ritard.
A♭7
G7

DORIAN MODE

The Blues sometimes derives its unique sound by using tones from special scales called *modes*. One of them is the **Dorian mode,** created centuries ago. The D Dorian mode, shown below, uses all the white notes from D to D. Blues players frequently use modes in their music to vary the mood and intensity of a composition.

The Dorian Mode (scale) contains a flatted 3rd and 7th as compared to a Major Scale.

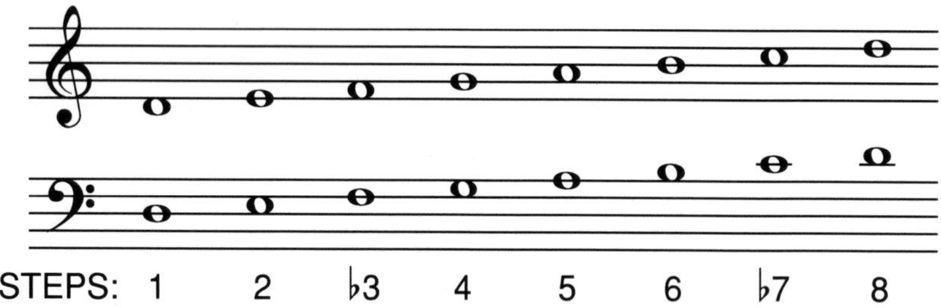

Down Below

Here's a short piece to practice using the **D Dorian mode** in both right and left hands.

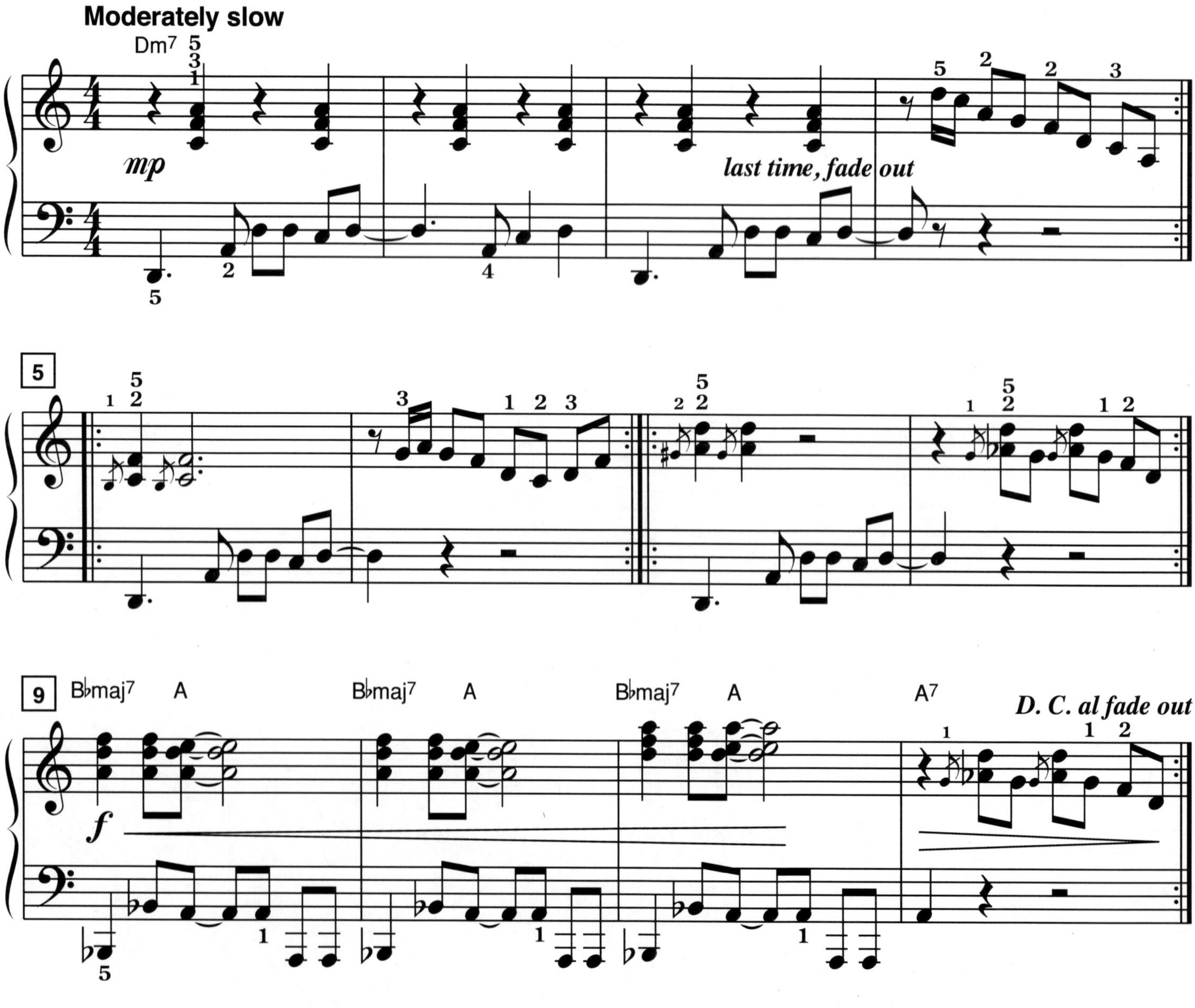

Moderately slow

Dm7

mp

last time, fade out

5

9 B♭maj7 A B♭maj7 A B♭maj7 A A7

f

D. C. al fade out

Dorian Mode Performance Piece

Time For a Change Blues

This piece uses a dramatic change in tempo (at measure 7) along with the special sounds of the Dorian mode to create a real rocker!

Track 39

C Dorian Mode Performance Solo

Inner City

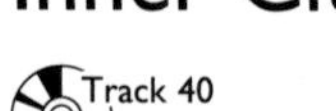

Moderately slow (Jazz Style)

Cm | Dm7(♭5) G7(♭5) | Cm | D7 G7

mp

5 Cm | Fm7 A♭maj7 | Cm | Fm7 Gm C

9 Fm7 | | Cm7 |

f–p *p–pp*

13 G7 | | (Rock Style) Cm |

f–p

17

mf *RH 8va bassa on repeat*

21
25
p–pp
29
G
p
mp
mf
f
gliss.
(Jazz Style)
33
Cm
Dm7(♭5)
G7(♭5)
Cm
D7
G7
mp
Cm
Fm7
A♭maj7
Cm7
Fm7
Cm
37
very slowly

Blues Jam

The Moon Has Two Faces Blues

The A, B♭ and F Dorian modes, bluesy sounds and blues scale tones heaped over a walking bass line and re-voiced chords are all features to produce a blues that is as fascinating as the many faces of the moon.

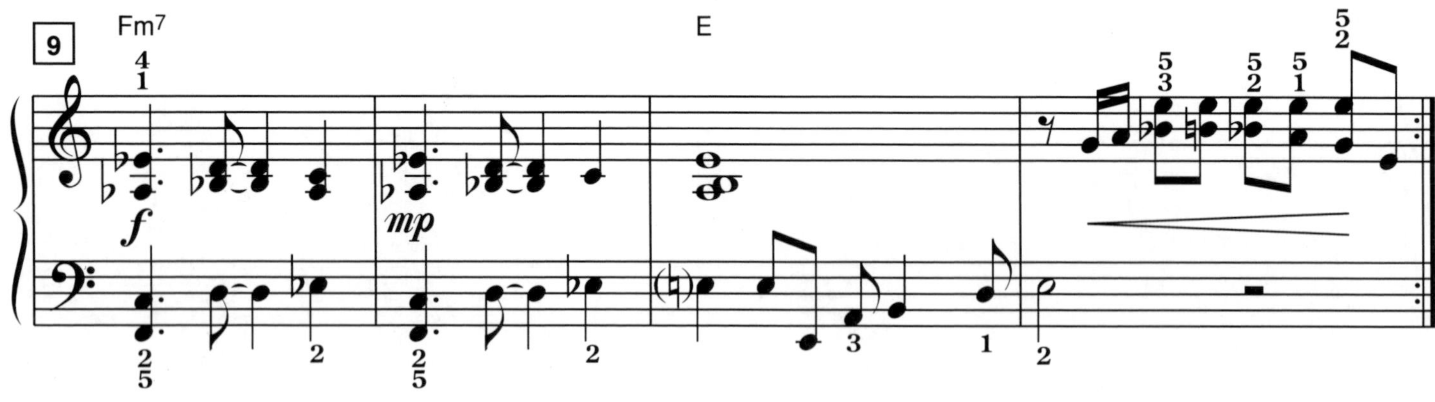

F7
C7
G
F7
C
E7
Am7
mp
Fm7
E
f–p
Am
p–pp
ritard. last time
B♭m7
(fermata
last time)

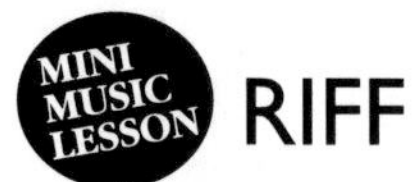

MINI MUSIC LESSON RIFF

A **Riff** is a short, repeated musical idea around which a composition is organized. It creates musical energy and excitement and is often the part of a piece that is most remembered. Riffs can be developed around a melodic idea (measures 1–8), or a rhythmic pattern (measures 9–16).

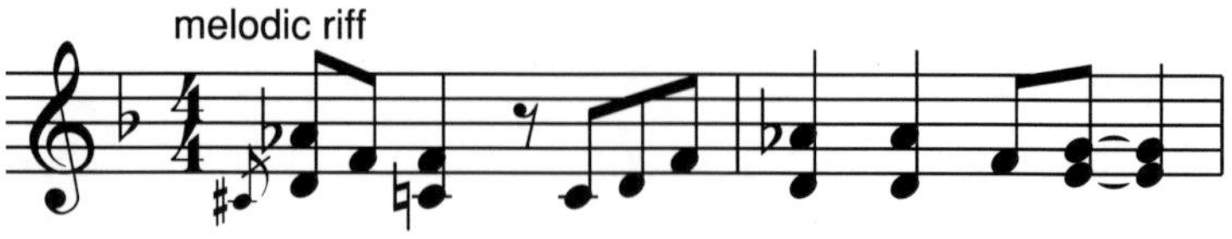
melodic riff

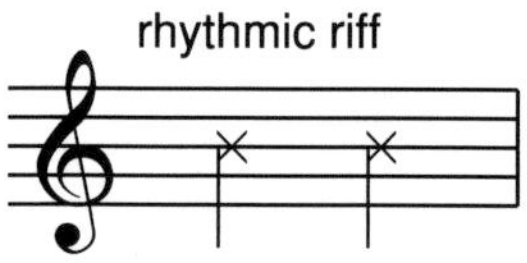
rhythmic riff

Short Timer

Track 42

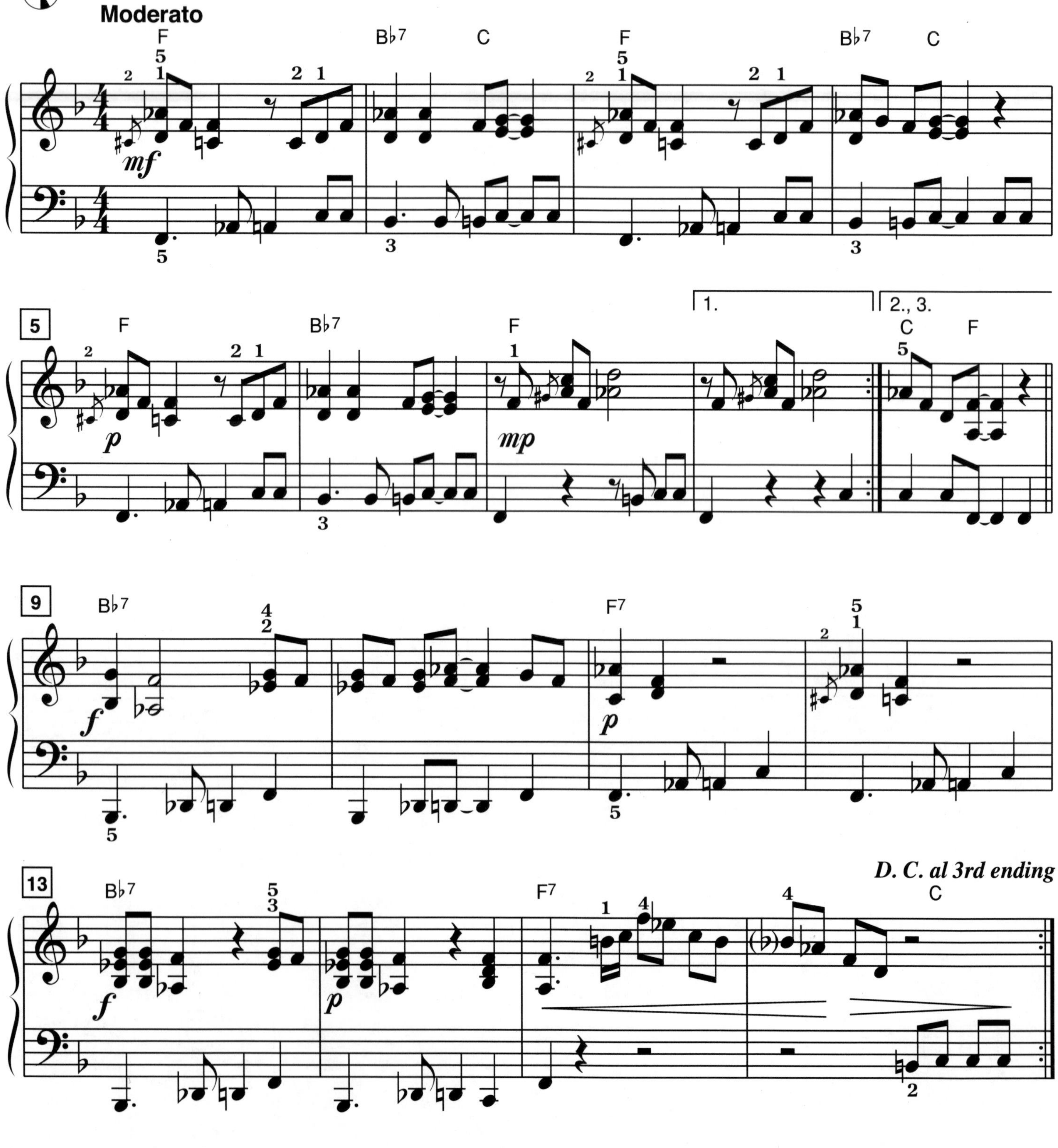
Moderato
F
B♭7
C
mf
p
mp
1.
2., 3.
F7
f
D. C. al 3rd ending

Riff Performance Piece with Left-Hand Latin Rhythm

Latin Quarter Blues

The Latin rhythms in the left hand should be played in a legato (smooth), lyrical manner so that the riff in the right hand can be heard clearly.

Relaxed and moving

Cm7 D D♭ N.C.

mf–p *f*

5 Cm Cm7 Cm Cm7

mp–mf

9 Fm Fm7 Cm

mf–f

13 A♭7 G7 Cm Cm7 Cm

f–p *D. C. al Fine* *Fine* *pp*

The B♭ Blues Scale

The key of B♭ is used a good deal in the Blues, especially when a sax and trumpet are added. Practice the complete B♭ Blues Scale, paying particular attention to the fingering.

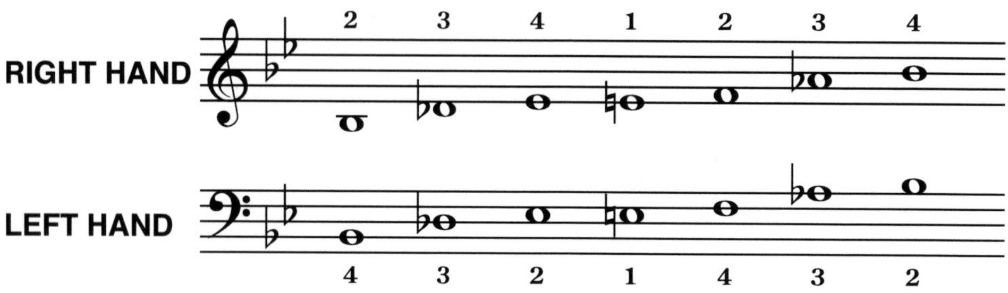

Now practice **B♭ Etudes #1** and **#2,** beginning slowly and working up to a moderate speed.

B♭ Etude #1

B♭ Etude #2

Optional: Play **B♭ Etudes #1** and **#2** (then return to **#1**) to make a complete piece.

B♭ Blues Scale Performance Piece

Goin' Home

This Blues should be played in a very determined manner, with a strong beat. Learn some of the special blues "licks" (RH measures 2, 4, 6 and 13–14). Try incorporating them into your own Blues.

Track 44

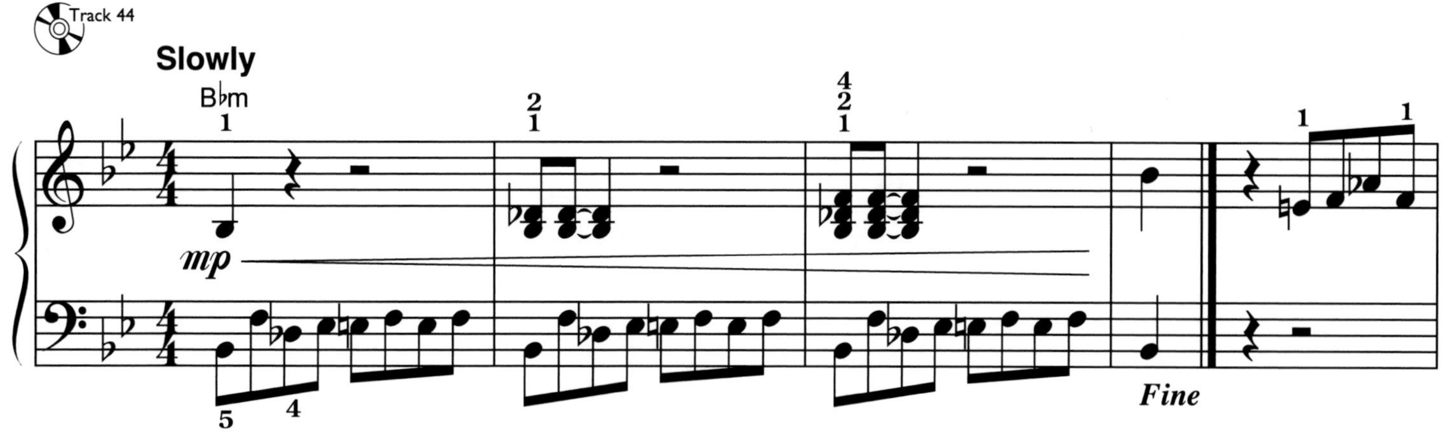

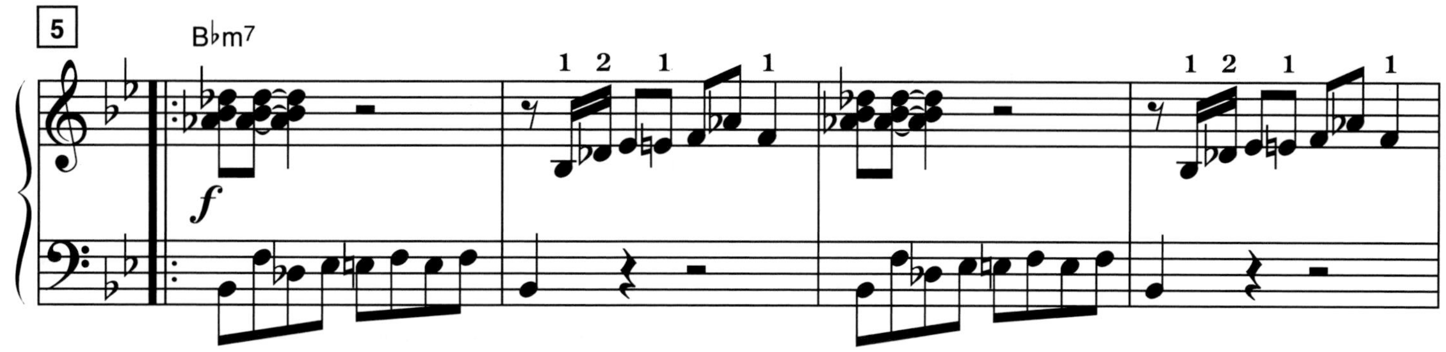

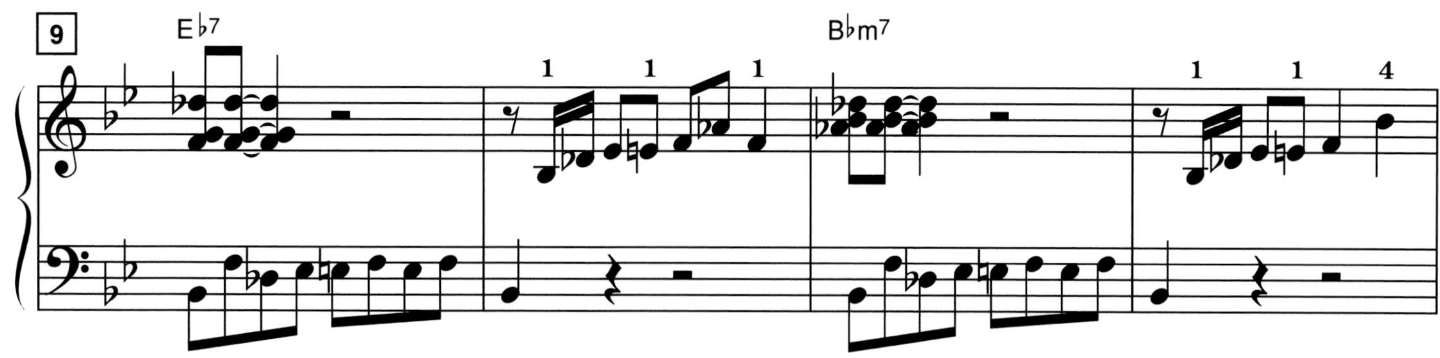

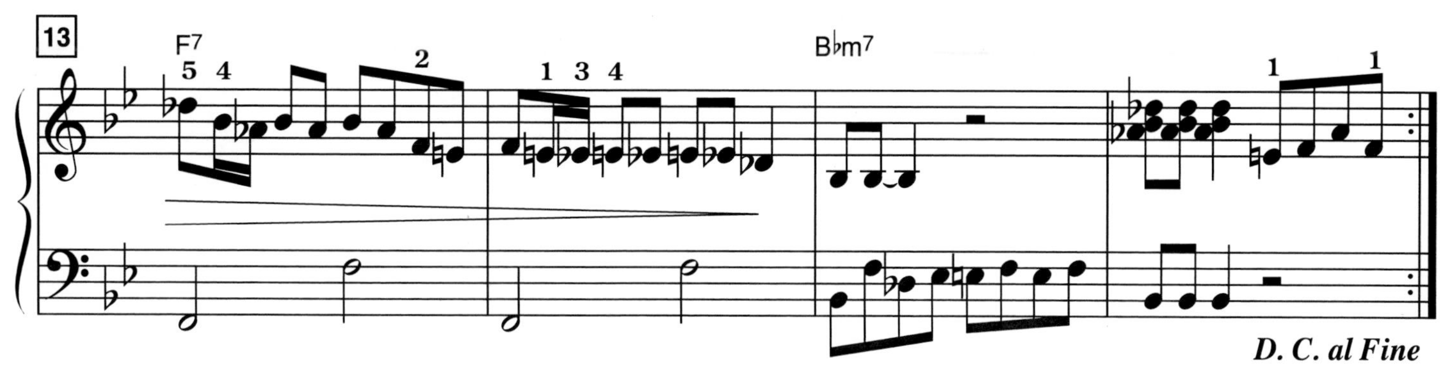

Single-Line Riff in B♭

Boiling Point

A riff often becomes the main idea of a piece of music. Its frequent repetition in a piece adds a forceful rhythmic punch. Riffs make the playing really hot.

Track 45

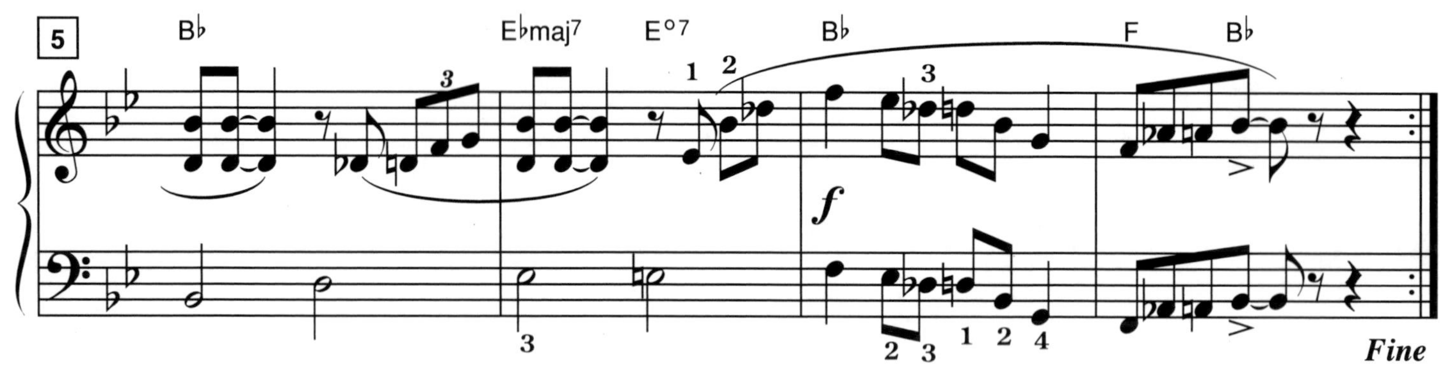

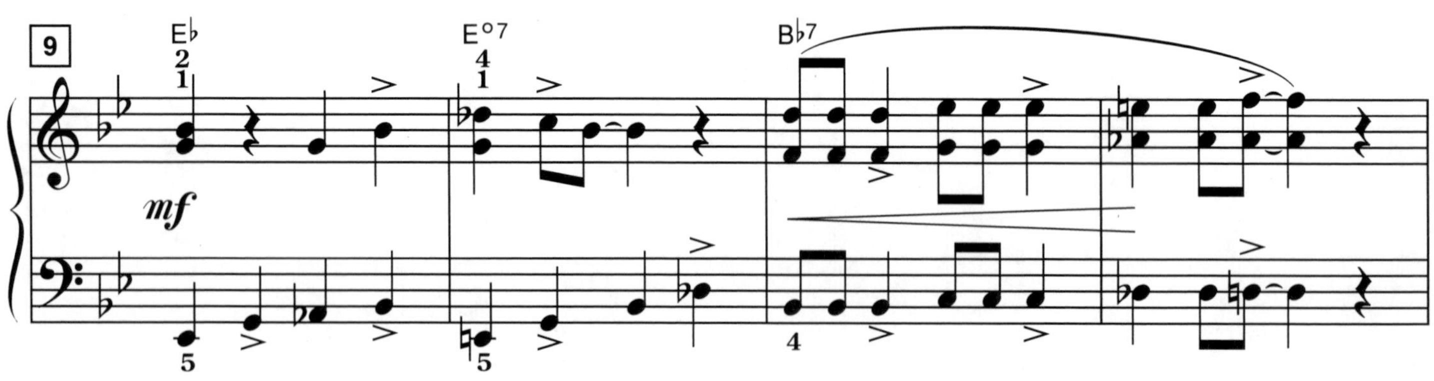

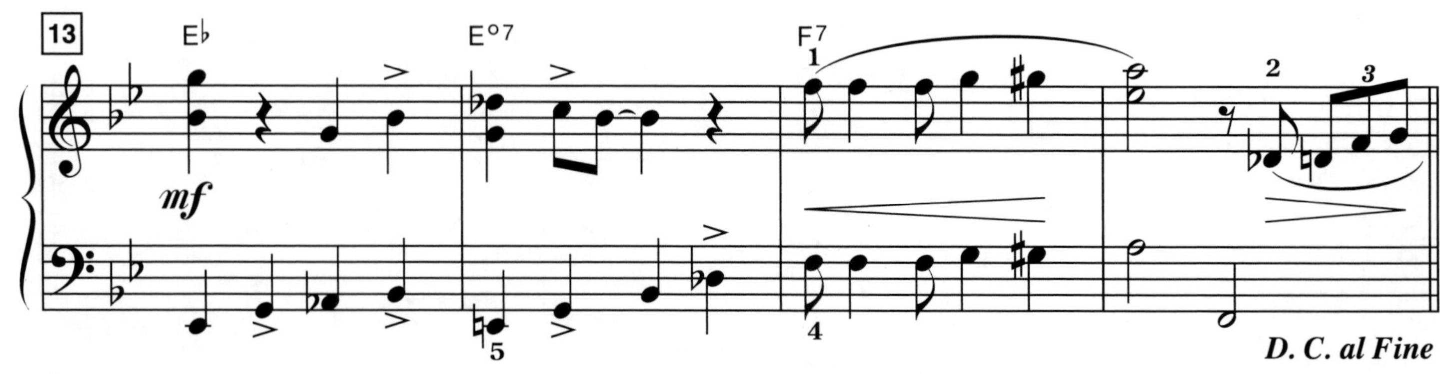

Chordal Riff in B♭

Convertible Blues

Riffs may be created from single line or chordal motifs. **Boiling Point** (page 74) and **Convertible Blues** may be played as one complete piece. Begin with **Boiling Point**, continue on to **Convertible Blues** and end with **Boiling Point**.

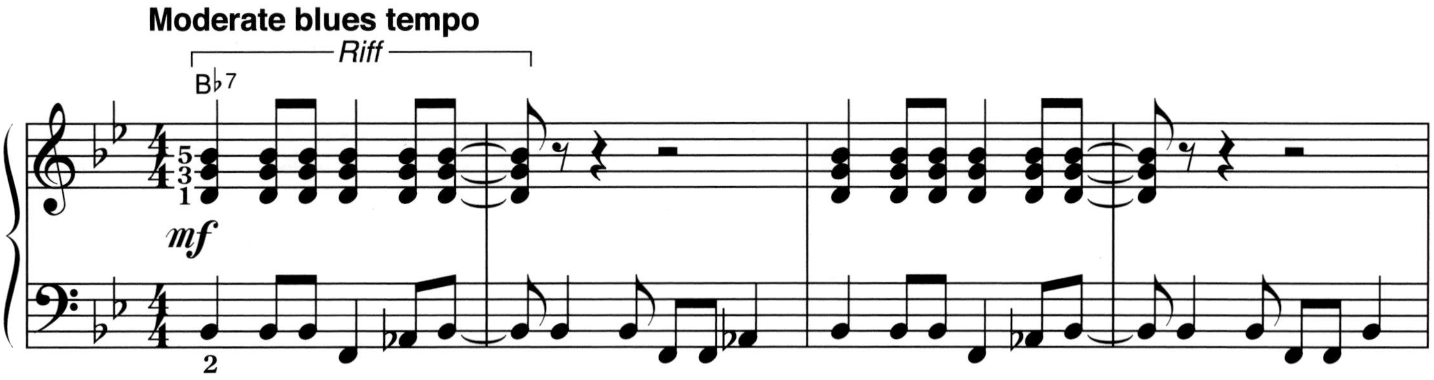

Moderate blues tempo

Riff

B♭7

mf

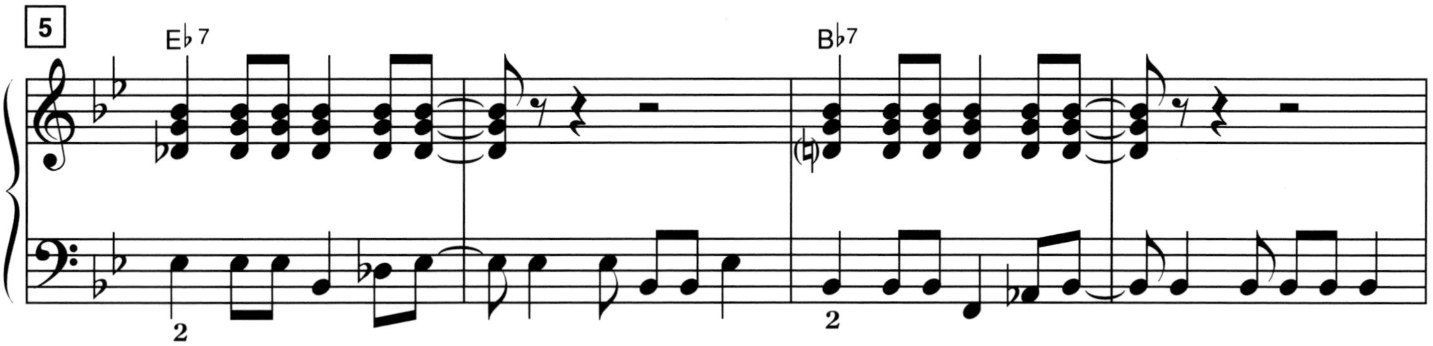

5

E♭7

B♭7

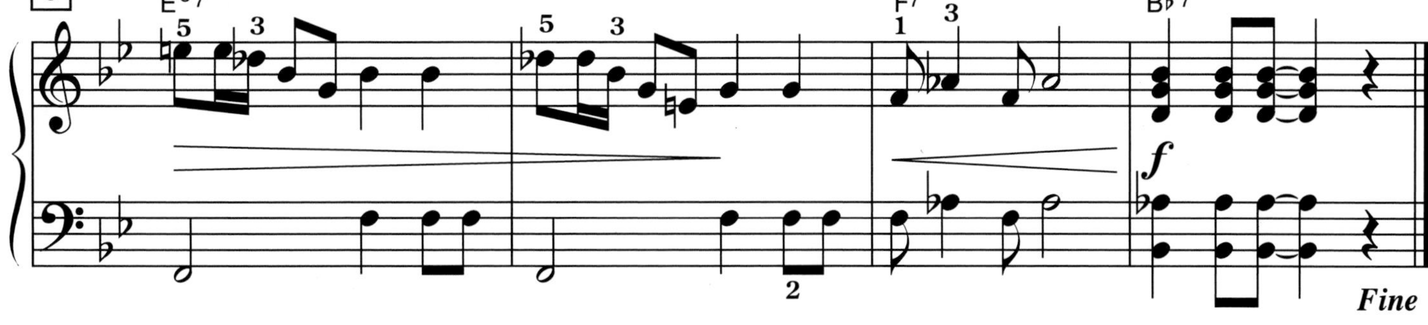

Improv section

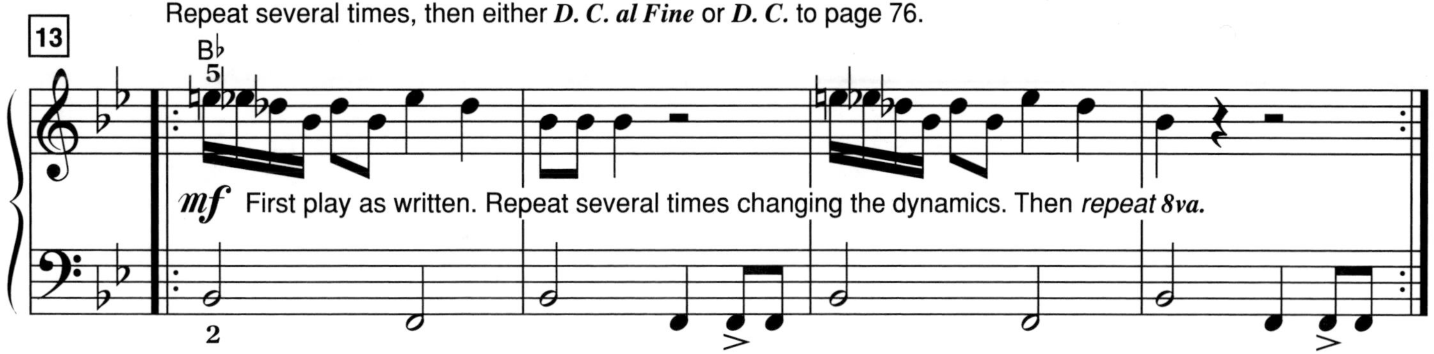

Single-Line and Chordal Riffs in B♭ Performance Piece

2nd Chance Blues

This Blues gives you a chance to add your musical ideas to a written composition. Add a new feeling to these riffs by improvising with changing *dynamics* (loud & soft) and *registration* (high & low) when you repeat each section. The sections are measures 1–12 and 29–36.

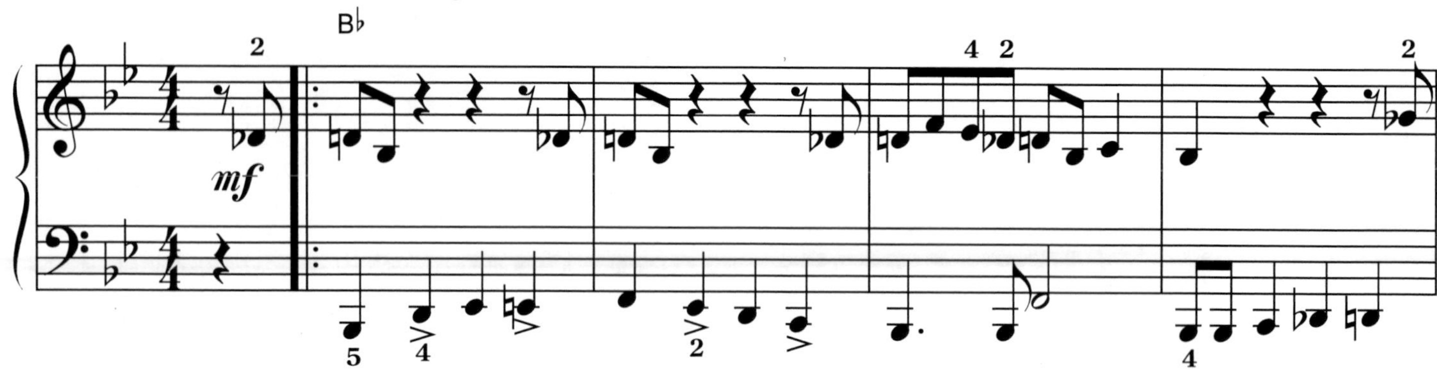

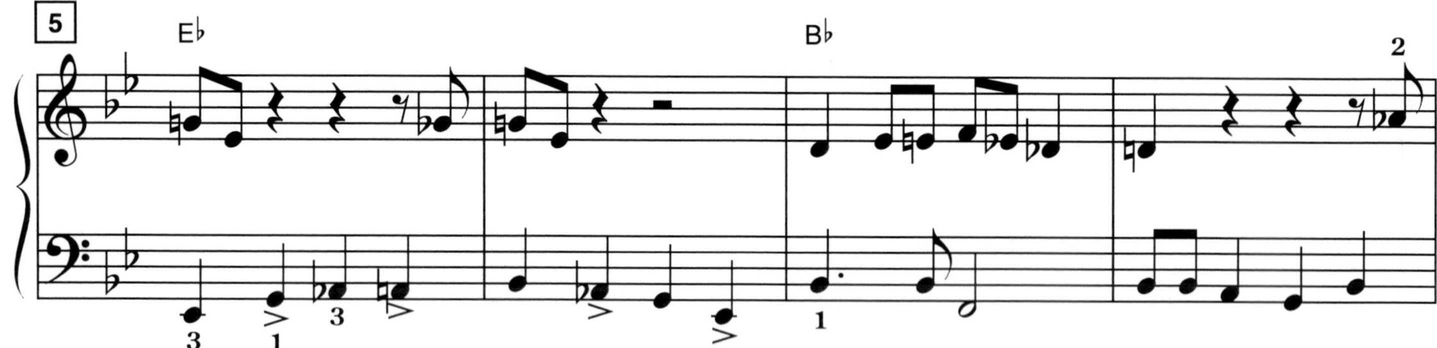

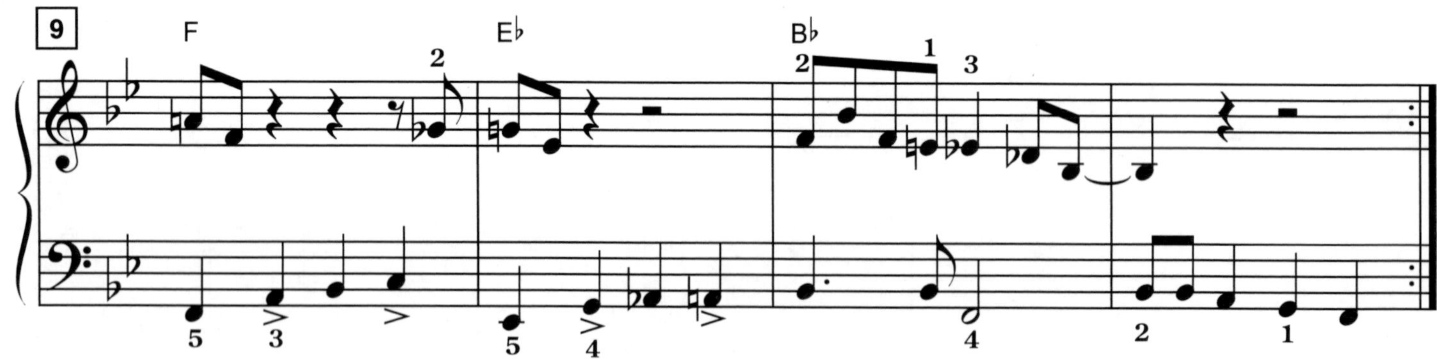

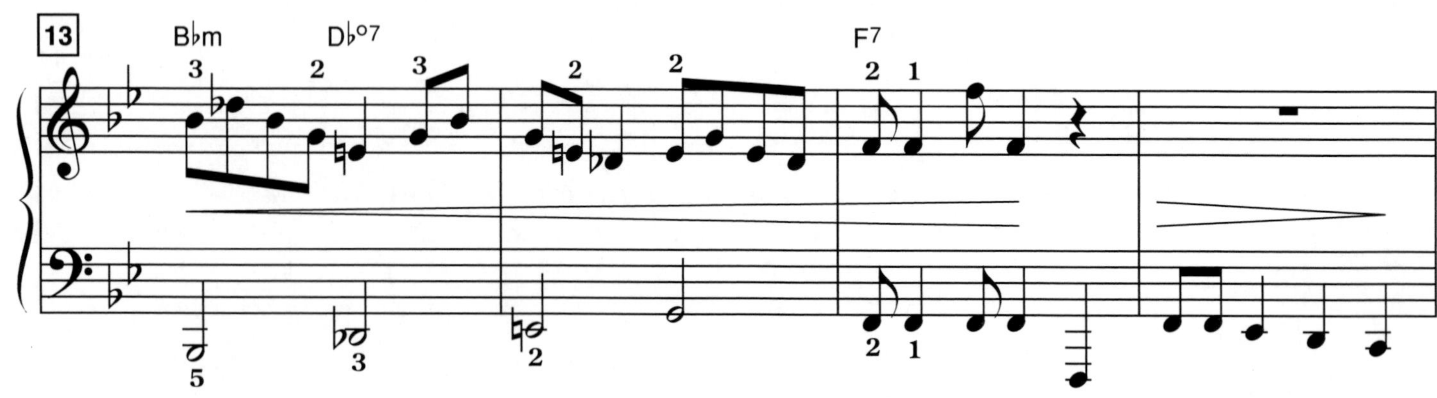

17
B♭7
mf
21
E♭7
B♭7
25
E°7
F7
29
B♭
f
E♭7
E°7
B♭
Gm
F7
33
B♭
E♭7
E°7
B♭
F7
1.
2.
8va
B♭

CHORD DICTIONARY

Chord Symbols are used to help keyboard players add harmony to the melody and "fake" the left-hand accompaniments. Here are some of the basic chords, many of which are used in this book.

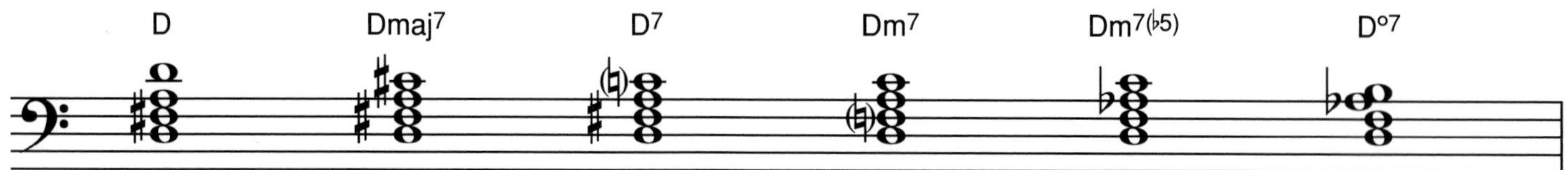

STEVE WINWOOD

Keyboardist Steve Winwood, who started performing in his early teens with the R&B band *The Spencer Davis Group*, still uses the foundation of the blues in his session work and his own illustrious solo career.

JERRY LEE LEWIS

As one of the founders of rock 'n' roll, Jerry Lee Lewis took blues scales and progressions to new levels in his ground-breaking piano playing.

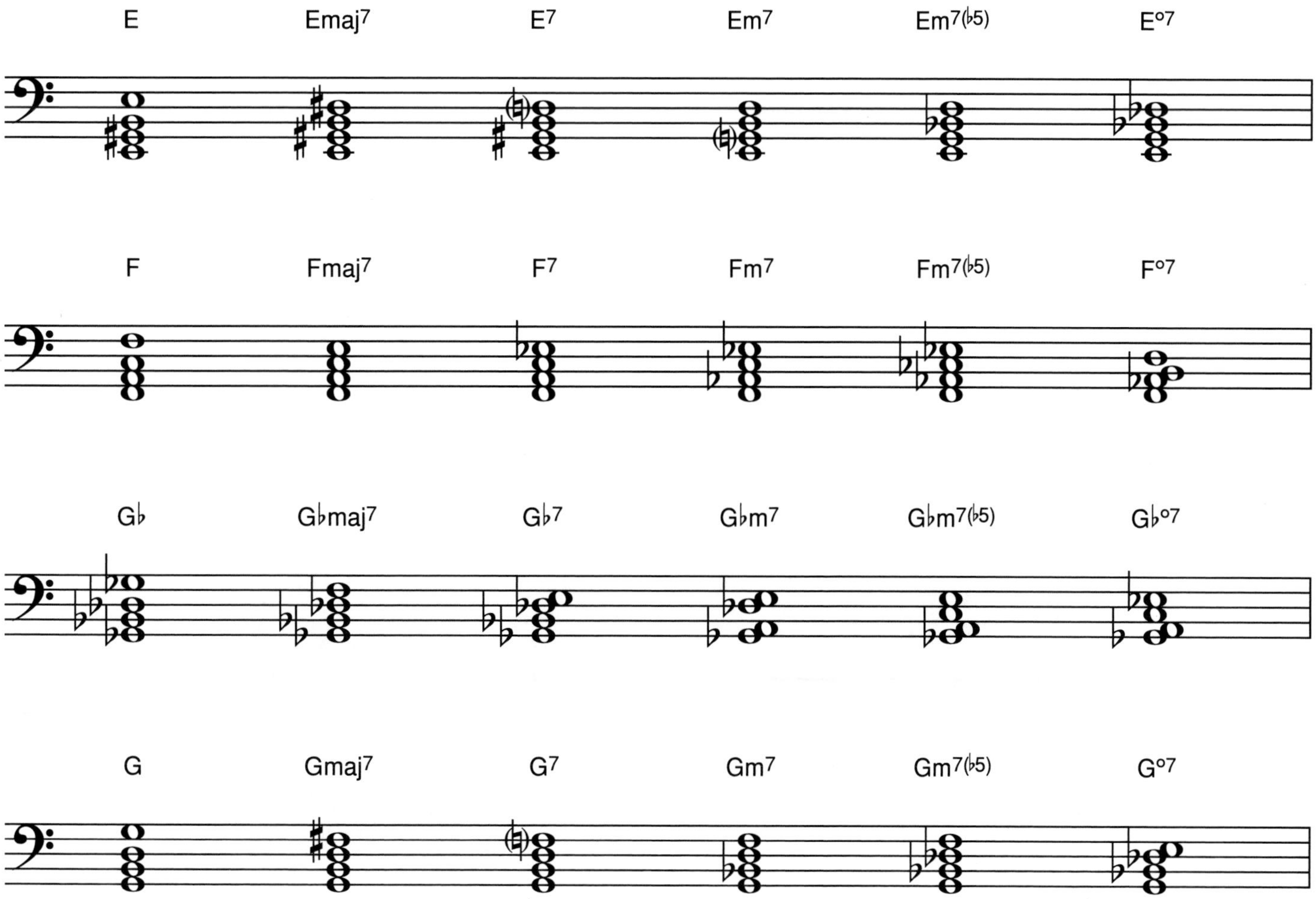

E Emaj7 E7 Em7 Em7(♭5) E°7

F Fmaj7 F7 Fm7 Fm7(♭5) F°7

G♭ G♭maj7 G♭7 G♭m7 G♭m7(♭5) G♭°7

G Gmaj7 G7 Gm7 Gm7(♭5) G°7

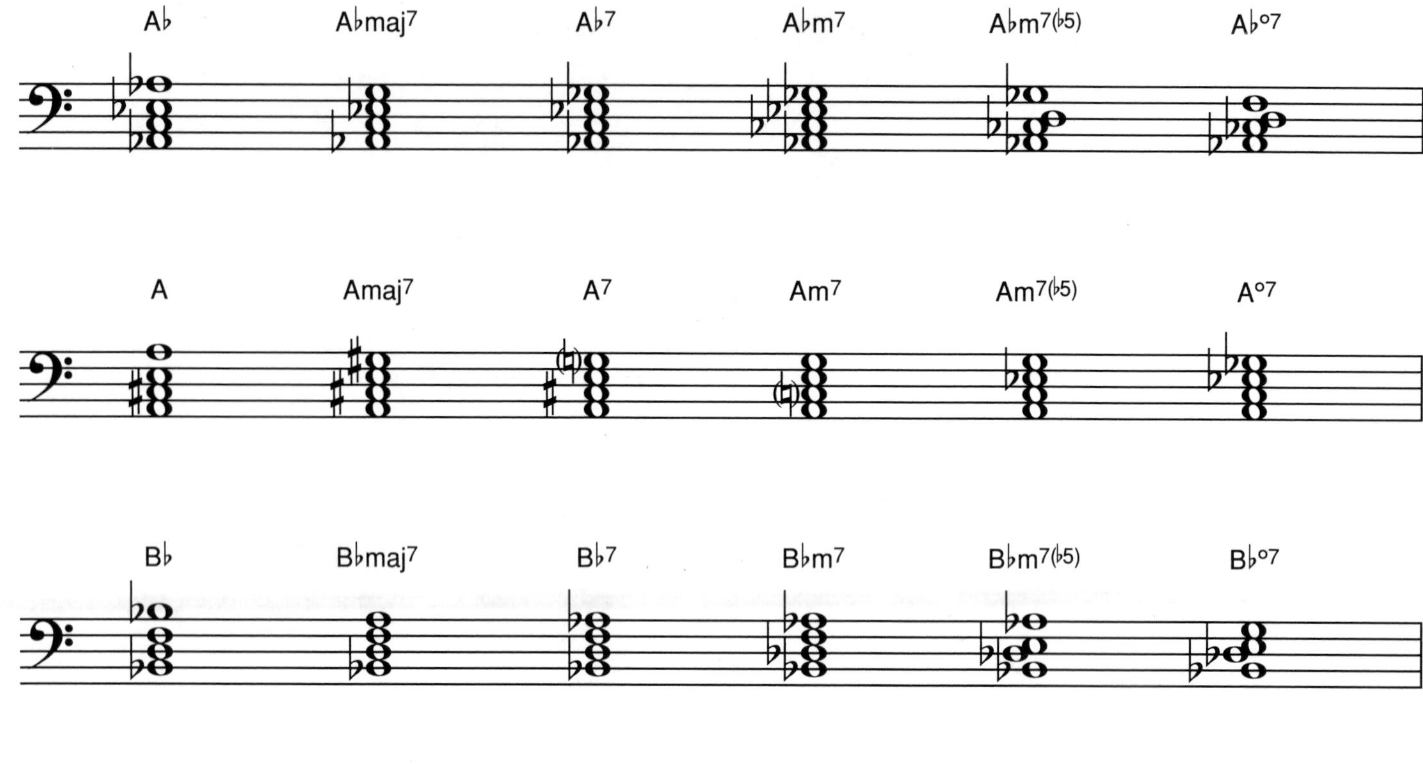
A♭
A♭maj7
A♭7
A♭m7
A♭m7(♭5)
A♭°7
A
Amaj7
A7
Am7
Am7(♭5)
A°7
B♭
B♭maj7
B♭7
B♭m7
B♭m7(♭5)
B♭°7

B
Bmaj7
B7
Bm7
Bm7(♭5)
B°7